William F. Kraft, PhD

Ways of the Desert

Becoming Holy Through Difficult Times

Pre-publication REVIEWS, COMMENTARIES, EVALUATIONS . . .

"Kraft's book holds out no false promises and guarantees no easy times for the spirit's journey. This is not a book of fast-food spirituality nor a book of pull-yourself-up-by-your-own-bootstraps advice. On the contrary, Kraft shows us that 'it is a mistake to assume that the desert is a bad place to be and that God is not with us.' The desert of our spiritual journey through life blooms with the crisis of both life and death, limit and possibility, loss and gain, past and future.

This is a beautiful book of the spirit and for the spirit. It is a thoughtful book that can change your life. There are no quick fixes, no magic solutions, no panaceas to solve the agonizing and glorious journey through the desert.

Kraft encourages us to be not afraid, but to face negative emotions head on and to find in them the challenge and opportunity for spiritual growth. From a psychological perspective, anxiety, depression, fear, loneliness, and guilt can be seen as disruptive psychic conditions, churning up inner turmoil and distress. From a spiritual perspective, these same emotions can be understood as challenges to growth and invitations to deepen our life of the spirit.

In this book you will find no counterfeits of the spirit, but solid food for the journey. There is no pablum for children here but words of life. Kraft teaches us how to tap into our desert moments of negative affectivity for the waters of life."

David L. Smith, CSSp, STL, PhD
Executive Director,
Simon Silverman
Phenomenology Center,
Duquesne University,
Pittsburgh, PA

More pre-publication
REVIEWS, COMMENTARIES, EVALUATIONS . . .

"*Ways of the Desert* is a book that can comfort people who are looking for guidance with the problems they are facing in their daily lives. The advantage of this book is that it grants the reader a basic insight into the problem of suffering and its place in our spiritual development through the use of practical and understandable references to everyday experiences. Kraft weaves his ideas around the image or symbol of the desert, which he believes can lead to promised lands of healthy and holy growth. Moreover, he does not stop at these general principles but works them out in detail by describing what he calls desert languages. Then he relates what he has described to different stages of human development. This book is most useful for all of us who are sharing the spiritual journey. Many people in all stages of life can profit from this work that offers light and consolation in difficult times."

Adrian van Kaam, CSSp, PhD
Professor of Formation Theology,
Epiphany Academy
of Formative Spirituality,
Pittsburgh, PA

"*Ways of the Desert* is a radical perspective on the developmental process in that it goes to the essence of human unfolding. The spiritual perspective, rather than simply adding one more viewpoint to human growth, re-orders our vision while inviting us to transcend societal definitions of the 'successful life.'

Using the language of the desert—the place of transformation from a condition of servitude to the fullness of life—Kraft demonstrates clearly how life's transitions are in the service of growth in freedom. The reader feels a call to engage fully in the process of authentic living rather than escaping into passing distractions and comforts.

By weaving the thread of the spiritual desert into the tapestry of human development from young adulthood to the elder years, Kraft transforms current theory, awakens possibilities, and restores meaning to human existence."

Martha LeGates, PhD
Adjunct Associate Professor,
Carlow College;
Psychotherapist and Supervisor,
Adult Outpatient Turtle Creek Valley,
Pittsburgh, PA

More pre-publication
REVIEWS, COMMENTARIES, EVALUATIONS . . .

"In *Ways of the Desert,* William F. Kraft presents what it means to experience a mature, adult spirituality in our postmodern age. He skillfully reveals the transformative possibilities that we may discover in what we ordinarily consider to be negative, unhealthy experiences: anxiety, depression, loneliness, and loss of meaning, to name a few. Kraft shows how the 'desert' experiences (crises, life transition) in young, middle, and late adulthood can lead to a new, transformed, meaningful life if we grasp the paradoxical and contradictory nature of human existence.

Kraft adeptly captures this essential yet often misunderstood structure of healthy, adult spiritual experiences. As a phenomenologist, he initially sets aside traditional theological presuppositions to help the reader 'see' with a different wholesome perspective how one can reconcile the contradictions in psychological/spiritual crises: how loneliness can be seen as a desire for greater love; how despair can be transformed into deeper hope; how one's doubts can lead to an even stronger faith, and how the loss of meaning can lead to a deeper wisdom.

Although it does not exclude wholesome piety, this is not a pious explanation of our human struggle. It is the work of a mature existential phenomenologist who creatively integrates psychology and spirituality. This book will become a solid guide for contemporary psychologists, counselors, teachers, and parents who often deal with these psychospiritual issues. This is a must-read for persons who want insight into a well-grounded postmodern psychospirituality seen from the existential phenomenological perspective."

Fr. Vernon Holtz, OSB, PhD
Chairperson,
Psychology Department,
Saint Vincent College,
Latrobe, PA

"Dr. Kraft has done it again. Throughout his career he has skillfully integrated the insights of psychology and spirituality without collapsing one into the other, and without acquiescing to a trendy 'vibration' spirituality evident in so much contemporary writing.

For this reader, the lynchpin of his new book has to be his treatment of 'desert languages' in Chapter 4. He makes the subtle yet necessary distinctions between our psychological and spiritual interpretations of experience and emerges with a 'desert hermeneutics' rooted in the paradox of desert language. As a result, the reader is empowered by the rich mystical desert tradition and, along with it, the language that 'knows' that a successful negotiation of human existence requires a 'dark light' and a 'light darkness.'

Serious students of Christian spirituality will benefit from Dr. Kraft's short but illuminating descriptions of our psychological life. But the book's primary appeal is twofold: (1) underlying the entire text is a desert spirituality that Dr. Kraft articulates not only skillfully but boldly; (2) Dr. Kraft writes in a style that will reach particularly, and hopefully, those uninitiated in the language of the desert.

This is a welcome book that will be especially helpful for those who have been led to believe that wandering in the desert of life is our only alternative. Dr. Kraft, while acknowledging that we cannot always control the life events that lead us into the desert, presents the reader with a means of wandering purposefully. If the deserts of life are inevitable, then so are the oases. Dr. Kraft helps us to find them."

John W. Alverson, PhD
Associate Professor of Theology,
Carlow College,
Pittsburgh, PA

NOTES FOR PROFESSIONAL LIBRARIANS AND LIBRARY USERS

This is an original book title published by The Haworth Pastoral Press, an imprint of The Haworth Press, Inc. Unless otherwise noted in specific chapters with attribution, materials in this book have not been previously published elsewhere in any format or language.

CONSERVATION AND PRESERVATION NOTES

All books published by The Haworth Press, Inc. and its imprints are printed on certified pH neutral, acid free book grade paper. This paper meets the minimum requirements of American National Standard for Information Sciences-Permanence of Paper for Printed Material, ANSI Z39.48-1984.

Ways of the Desert

Becoming Holy Through Difficult Times

William F. Kraft, PhD

The Haworth Pastoral Press
An Imprint of The Haworth Press, Inc.
New York • London • Oxford

Published by

The Haworth Pastoral Press, an imprint of The Haworth Press, Inc., 10 Alice Street, Binghamton, NY 13904-1580

Cover design by Marylouise E. Doyle.

Library of Congress Cataloging-in-Publication Data

Kraft, William F., 1938-
Ways of the desert : becoming holy through difficult times / William F. Kraft.
p. cm.
Includes bibliographical references and index.
ISBN 0-7890-0859-9 (alk. paper). — ISBN 0-7890-0860-2 (pbk. : alk. paper)
1. Spiritual life. 2. Adults—Religious life. I. Title.
BL624.K7515 1999
291.4′2—DC21 99-36498
CIP

To my family and friends—
Pilgrims in Deserts
and Promised Lands

ABOUT THE AUTHOR

William F. Kraft, PhD, is Professor of Psychology at Carlow Col lege in Pittsburgh, Pennsylvania. A local, national, and international lecturer, Dr. Kraft also has a private practice in psychological services and is a consultant to the Catholic Dioceses of Pittsburgh and Greensburg, Pennsylvania. The author of many books and articles including *The Normal Alcoholic, The Search for the Holy,* and *Whole and Holy Sexuality,* Dr. Kraft's writing primarily focuses on the area of integrating psychology and spirituality from an existential-phenomenological perspective.

CONTENTS

The Desert will lead you
to your Heart where
I will speak

Preface

Becoming holy is not easy. It involves difficult and challenging times—and enjoyable and effortless times. Spiritual journeys, like all good journeys, incorporate all the seasons—the dark discontent of winter, the promising emergence of spring, the restful light of summer, the comforting climax of fall. We are people of and for all seasons.

Good souls tell good stories. They are permeated with light and darkness, presence and absence, joy and sadness, strength and weakness, life and death. Such apparent contradictions make for good stories and for good living. Any other way is an illusion.

Yet we often act as if we have one (usually the more comfortable) without the other. Pursuing false promises of fulfillment, we futilely try to be enlightened without darkness, to rejoice without sadness, to be intimate without loneliness, to be strong without weakness, to arrive without being lost.

While helping and learning from clients and colleagues, I discovered that "negative" experiences such as loneliness, depression, and anxiety can be opportunities for positive growth. I listened to desert languages—loneliness, aloneness, depression, anxiety, fear, guilt, shame, frustration, anger, boredom, apathy, and anguish. Instead of judging such experiences as symptomatic of unhealthiness, I explored how they may lead to health. I discovered how depression can lead to joy, how anxiety can help us attain serenity, and how loneliness can be a harbinger of love. Instead of being depressed about being depressed, anxious about being anxious, and guilty about being lonely, new possibilities emerged from these difficulties. I learned that deserts lead to promised lands.

Our thesis is that apparent opposites are necessary and related parts of healthy and holy growth—that especially in the spiritual life, the positive and negative are dialectically related. In most Western cultures, however, acceptance of this reality is not common, and its rejection engenders spiritual stagnation. While questioning the assumption that all uncomfortable feelings are harmful experiences to expunge, we will explore alternative ways to construe and cope with the paradoxical dynamics of spiritual development.

This book was written partly because original studies on spirituality and its relation to adult life cycle development are relatively rare. Important and popular authors such as Erikson, Levinson, Neugarten, Sheehy, Vaillant, and others deal mainly with the psychosocial dimensions of adulthood. And, with few exceptions, recent models of spiritual development are also based on psychosocial perspectives. Indeed, such studies are valuable to understanding adult development as well as learning how to manage stress. In short, our concern—a spiritual vision of adult development—is rarely addressed explicitly.

The proposed model incorporates, to various degrees, many authors, and I am indebted to them. From a psychological viewpoint, theoretical and empirical studies of adult development influenced my perspective. Classic and contemporary spiritual literature and phenomenological studies contributed even more significantly. Furthermore, personal journeys with friends, students, and clients generated a concrete appreciation for and a validation of life cycle processes. In fact, another impetus for writing this book was to respond to these sojourners' repeated declarations that "nothing makes sense." Finally, students and I conducted and analyzed more than a thousand interviews focused on developmental transitions with persons age eighteen to ninety-six.

No book is the product of one person. I thank Pat Frauenholz and Janine Geibel for their typing, and George Maloney for his support. I will always be grateful to patients, students, friends, and family who shared themselves with me and taught me that theory is in service of life. Both their light and dark experiences enlightened and inspired. Finally, I thank God for Life and Death and Life.

Chapter 1

Desert Stories

Nothing makes sense. So many questions. So many ways of looking at things. Sometimes I think I have the answer, but then things change again. It seems the more answers I get, the more questions there are. So many ways; what's my way? Will I find the answer?

Life used to go well. Nothing seemed to bother me like it does now. I know I can't go back to the way it was, yet I don't know where I'm going. It's as if I'm no longer back there and not yet out there. I feel empty inside, and it scares me. I'm at a loss. I don't know what it is. Is it me? What's going on?

Sometimes I feel hemmed in, trapped. I'm stuck and I don't want to be stuck. When it really gets tough, I feel leveled, almost paralyzed. It takes extra effort to move myself, and for what? Am I clinically depressed? I function well enough to get by. But function for what? I'm tired of struggling. Tired of trying to make sense of my life. And I'm tired of being tired.

God? I used to think there was a God, but now I'm not so sure. God certainly doesn't make the same sense; in fact, I wonder if God makes any sense. What kind of God would leave me so alone and lonely? When I reach out, I end up with nothing in my grasp. For years, I tried to live according to God's standards, and what am I left with? Nothing!

Maybe God is a figment of our collective imagination. Maybe we were taught to believe in God as a way to control ourselves and keep social order. Who knows—without God there might be chaos. Maybe Freud was right; maybe God is a mental construct—an illusion. I hope not. I hope there is a God who can help me make sense.

> If there is a God, why is there so much suffering? So much injustice? So much evil? What good does it do to live a good life, and then get crapped on? Sometimes it seems that bad people do better than good people. God: Where are you? Who are you? What kind of a God are you? Do you really exist? And if you do, what good are you? Hello! Are you there, God?
>
> Sure, I don't always feel this way. Yet, even in my so-called good times I feel restless, like something is missing. I feel there must be more to life. I see other people who seem to be content, who don't seem to be experiencing what I'm going through. I feel like some sort of oddball. Yet I don't want to be simply content. Cows are content. Life must mean more than this.
>
> I feel so lonely. I wonder if I'll ever get close to someone. When I *do* reach out to someone, it doesn't seem to work out. I always seem to end up where I started—by myself. What's the sense if you are alone? So often, when I'm by myself in my room, I feel as if I'm trapped in a tall, dark cylinder. I can see the light at the top, but I can't seem to climb out. I keep falling back to the bottom where it's dark and silent. I feel alone—so alone.

Is this woman suffering from clinical depression, or can there be other ways of interpreting her experiences? For instance, instead of being indicative of "bad" times, could she be undergoing a difficult passage that leads to better times? Could her experience of nothingness be a prelude to making more sense? Could her depths of depression lead to greater heights of joy? Instead of being symptomatic of psychopathology, could her experience be necessary for spiritual growth? Actually, too little data is given for a differential diagnosis. However, there is more than one possibility.

There are more ways than one to construe an experience. Actually, there is a spectrum of meaning. Such experiences may be symptomatic of pathology, or they may be symptomatic of healthy growth. And our experience can be a mixture of both healthy and less than healthy components. Too often, however, we automatically interpret such experiences as negative, rather than patiently discerning what the experience means. With good intentions, we can mistakenly call healthy experiences unhealthy.

Not infrequently, psychological and psychiatric perspectives construe such experiences as pathological, less than healthy, or at least suspect. But from a spiritual perspective, such experiences may be necessary and healthy. Actually, it is very difficult, if not impossible, to grow spiritually without experiences of nothingness, powerlessness, and meaninglessness. Without experiencing the absence of others, it is difficult to grow in intimacy—and to be consoled without desolation is a fiction. From a spiritual perspective, this woman may be healthy and on her way to becoming holier.

Our proposal is that all people suffer this so-called desert of nothingness. No one, however, experiences deserts exactly the way this woman did, but in ways that are influenced by their own nature and nurture. We all stand uniquely on the same desert ground of nothingness.

> Being around the halfway point of my life, I'm wondering. Do I want to continue to live as I have lived? And if not, then how? In spite of my irritation with work and competition, I have been very successful. I'm grateful for the income I'm making; it gives me and my family many things and opportunities. Still, it is very difficult to be professionally successful and live a meaningful personal life. I wonder about my marriage. Are my wife and I closer than when we were first married? I wonder if my kids really know me and if I know them. I get the feeling that they would rather have my personal presence more than my material presents. I know I did with my father.
>
> I am not unhappy, but there is something missing—something very important. Did I miss the boat? What is the boat? Is there a better way of living? There must be. Indeed, I live a good life, but . . . can I change my life? If there is more to life, then what is it? And how can I do it? So many questions, so few answers.
>
> Although my health is good, I wonder about death. I could live another forty years, but I've known people who have died at my age. Death seems closer to me now. Although I don't feel old, neither do I feel young. It's just that when I die, I

don't want to regret my life. I want to be able to say "yes" to life without regrets. I want to be able to say that I've lived a good life, written a good story, run the good race.

What about God, church, religion? I go to church every Sunday and really don't commit any serious sins. I try to be a good person. Still, I get uneasy when I think about my spiritual life. Deep within, I feel that there is a lot missing. If there really is a God, if there really is an afterlife, if we are put on earth to ultimately be in heaven, then what am I doing to live this kind of vision? Do I really live in the presence of God? Is my reason for being ultimately spiritual? And if so, what am I willing to do about it? And if there is no God or spiritual life, then what are the consequences of that? I think these kinds of questions are important, but they make me uneasy.

Sometimes I get kind of depressed or down. Am I clinically depressed or a candidate for chemotherapy? I don't think so. Still, I feel an emptiness, a lack of meaning, energy, and purpose in life. Life can get dark or at least gray. The light of the past no longer seems as relevant. Will there be light? Although I kind of believe that this dark night will lead to daylight, what kind of a day will it be?

I feel that my soul is searching for more. Too often, I respond to my thirst by drinking alcohol. The alcohol numbs my restlessness and fills my emptiness, but I know that my comfort is only temporary. Furthermore, my drinking doesn't seem to lead anywhere and, in fact, it hurts me. Still, what is there to fill the hole in my soul? Booze is not the answer. Although comforting, sex doesn't quite hit the bull's-eye. Religion helps, but it also falls short. What is an adequate answer to my questions?

Such midlife deserts are not uncommon. Some people would say that they are necessary for healthy development. As this successful businessman points out, it is easy and tempting to numb the pain of desert emptiness and to satisfy the thirst of desert seeking with alcohol, sexuality, or work. He points out that even religion is inadequate. It seems as if this man is searching for something that goes beyond the earth. We will see that such a depression is not clinical or pathological, but is a spiritual loss and powerlessness that can lead to significant gain and freedom. We will see that being lost in the desert can lead to being found revitalized.

The desert excludes no one. Think of this seventy-two-year-old woman:

> I don't know what's happening to me. I thought things were going pretty well, that life was set, and I guess it is. My kids are raised and doing well. My husband is in fairly good health and seems well, or at least content. But me, I don't know how I feel. Things were going all right for me, but lately nothing makes the same sense.
>
> I feel old and yet not old. I look at younger generations, and I feel old or that I should feel old. And yet, inside I still feel young. My old self wonders where my life has gone. Sometimes, I feel as if I've missed so many opportunities that I no longer have. Sure, I know that I've raised a good family and I've had a decent marriage, but there are so many other things that I didn't do and would like to have done. I don't know. When I start thinking and feeling this way, I can really get down. I can feel so darn inadequate. What have I really done? How much is life worth? Is there time left?
>
> My young self says there is time, but I know that time is running out. I could have twenty-five years or more, which is a lot of time. But the fact is that I've lived a lot longer than I have time left. My young self says, "Live!" My old self gets scared, tired, withdrawn. Still, my young self says, "Get up, move, and live until you die."
>
> It sounds silly, at least to me, but sometimes I really wonder who cares for me. I know that my husband and children do, but I don't feel it very much. I feel I've given more than I have received, and I still feel I give more than I receive. And I know it's stupid, but I feel guilty for feeling this way. Here I am in my seventies, and I feel lonely. I know people care for me, but I don't feel much of that care. Sometimes I feel like crying, but it doesn't seem to do any good. And then I feel silly, for I know they love me.
>
> I thought that once my children were out on their own, my husband and I could always do the things that we really

wanted to do. I thought that life would be better than ever and, in some ways, it is. But in other ways life, or at least my life, falls short. I feel so damn useless. Like I'm getting closer to death and there is something missing that I haven't achieved. Somehow life must mean more before I die. When I share some of these feelings with my husband and my kids, they tell me I shouldn't feel this way. They tell me to look at other older people and be grateful for what I have. Although this may seem harsh, they mean well. But they don't seem to understand. Does anyone understand?

I don't know when I will die. I do know that I'm not quite ready to die and that I have more living to do. But I'm not sure how and why to live the rest of my life. I know that I can live a good many years, but how and why do I want to live those years? When I'm on my deathbed, what will I be able to say about my life?

Listen to another veteran journeyer:

Yes, I'm glad you asked me. It seems that nobody wants to talk about dying, or about living. Since I am eighty-seven years old, I feel that I am an expert on both subjects. Indeed, I cannot escape death; it's too close to me. I can hear death outside my door and sometimes I'm tempted to hide. And yet, is death that bad? In a way, I look forward to death. This scares most people, but it no longer scares me. Maybe death is a harbinger of life. Maybe we will go out of this world like we came in.

When I think about my prenatal life and infancy, I have no recollection. And yet I know that I lived inside my mother's womb, that I initially appeared as one cell, then two cells, four, sixteen, and so on. I cannot remember that critical time for my development, but without it I would be nothing. Perhaps life after death is similar to life before death. Maybe we evolved out of nothingness and will continue to evolve after death. Maybe our being is perpetually becoming perfected. I know this may sound like philosophical gymnastics, but it makes sense to me. What can you expect from a retired professor?

I feel good that I can say that I really tried to live a good life. Far from perfection, indeed, but overall there was progress. I can say that when I was forty, I was a bit better than when I was twenty, and when I was sixty, I was a lot better than when I was forty. It seemed that the older I got, the better I got. And I'm glad to say that. And I can say that I never intentionally tried to hurt anyone for any extended period of time. *That* I'm proud of. And I always tried to help people, although to a fault. My so-called codependency got me into some trouble, but it was done out of love. Of course, there are some things that I'd change if I had to live over again—like spending more quality time with my spouse and children. But as I and they got older, we grew closer and enjoyed being together. Just like anyone else, I had some hard times; I was poor as a child. But I worked hard and found my way in life.

Sometimes I hurt. When I look outside my four walls and look at life going on out there, I wonder: I wonder about life and I wonder about death. My wife died five years ago and my children live some distance from me. Indeed, they come and visit me, but not very often and not for very long. They invite me to their house and that is pleasant. They are good kids, but they are of a different generation and have their own lives. Then I say, "Look, old man, you're too old to feel sorry for yourself. Life is too short to play the martyr role. Get up. Life is here. Live it."

When I see my new grandson, I know how old I am. I don't know if I'll see him grow to be a man and that's depressing. And yet strangely enough, I really don't mind too much. I know that this is part of life and, in a certain way, that it's good. Knowing that I don't have long to live urges me to live more fully. I am unlikely to take life for granted. I savor every moment.

I think of the past and sometimes dream of the past. Past experiences come vividly back and it's just like in *The Old Man and the Sea*. I relive my life. It's as if I'm watching a movie and the movie is on its last reel. But the movie is about me and, overall, I enjoy it. Sometimes I laugh; sometimes I cry. Sometimes I'm weak; sometimes I'm strong. Sometimes

> I'm empty; sometimes I'm fulfilled. In any case, it's a good movie. And the movie is coming to its climax.

This man is probably in his final desert and is coming to his final Promised Land. His positive attitude makes for a positive life. He seems motivated to live fully until he dies. He is able to accept the things he cannot change and to change the things he can. He avoids obsessing about life's absence and negativity, but rather focuses on and enjoys life's positive presence. His secret is simple: live until you die.

These kinds of experiences can be viewed as something to be avoided, treated, or purged. Professionally, they might be construed as unhealthy, negative, immature, or simply not addressed. Our contention is that these and similar desert experiences are essential to living a healthy and holy life. Consequently, it is wise to accept, attend to, learn from, and grow through them.

PILGRIM PEOPLE

All of us, whatever our age, are pilgrim people. We are perpetually on our way toward our reason for being—the ultimate promised land where there is no more pain and suffering, but rather perpetual peace and freedom. But while on earth, we never arrive. We are never fully content, secure, and happy; we only move forward in becoming content, secure, or happy. And therefore, we are always somewhat discontented, insecure, and unhappy. This is the nature of being on earth. Yet, in our age, when so many assume that complete self-fulfillment and self-control are possible to attain, we have difficulty accepting life as a pilgrimage that is interwoven with and beyond our desires and control.

Some of us assume that adulthood is the time when we should finally "arrive," when we should be "grown up." Such a static view is inaccurate. In fact, the opposite is true. Adulthood, like childhood and adolescence, is a time of dynamic growth. And, the older we become, the more unique we are. We are perpetual pilgrims.

Our approach is primarily spiritual—it includes deserts and promised lands. Consider deserts as life transitions—gifted times that pressure us to take radical stock of our lives. These critical times are opportunities that challenge us to move forward and/or retreat, to affirm and/or deny life, to grow and/or stagnate. Such a passage is a fork in the road and the road we choose is crucial. And, the road of spirituality is less traveled.

We may find it hard to believe that seemingly barren lands can give birth to new growth and nourish old growth. It may be difficult to accept that depression, loneliness, and anxiety may be necessary occasions for healthy and holy growth, yet such issues are typical of the desert.

When we assume that pain is usually indicative of something negative, we can sincerely take negative stands on what could be positive experiences. We can go through depressing times when we wonder what is "wrong" with ourselves and are unaware that such experiences could be necessary for spiritual growth. To be sure, all pain is not symptomatic of health. It can definitely indicate pathology and often does. Nevertheless, it is a popular illusion to assume that we can get to the land of milk and honey without going through dry and barren deserts.

So, to declare that loneliness is a good and necessary experience to be welcomed and cultivated, may sound stupid or sick. Let us not be so sure. Spiritual loneliness, for example, calls for deeper and more permanent love. In loneliness, we may be prepared to experience the presence of God in absence. Loneliness can keep us yearning for the Source of Love—Life's Spirit.

Consider that, in our healthy discontent, we are called to renew ourselves. Willingly or not, we no longer hold on to what once was. We desire new significance and seek to be freer—to grow and to become more than we have been. We can listen to the disconcerting but challenging call to become more than we have been, or we can silence its message, fixate, and regress.

Too easily, we forget our spiritual side and rely too much on what is physical and psychosocial. As a result, we become "normally mad." We are normal, insofar as we are reasonably adjusted and successful, and we behave within the confines of socially sanctioned norms. Consequently, we gain acceptance and earn certain rewards. Nevertheless, we are mad in that we are distant from spiritual experiences that are necessary for healthy and holy living. Despite our good intentions, we become too busy to reflect and pray, too tired to play and love, too preoccupied to listen, too controlled to surrender, and too self-sufficient to be saved.

Compounding matters is the cultural message to rely exclusively on ourselves to cope with our mortality. By stressing individualism and control, we find ourselves bound by our own limits. We are unaware of how to cope with and transcend our limits. "Transcendent dependency"—trusting God or a Higher Power—is often forgotten in the mad pursuit of independence and self-determination. The spiritual life invites us to recognize and humbly accept life as, ultimately, not in our hands. Grace—the essential force of spiritual growth—is a gift from God which is primarily given to those who surrender to God. God, not ourselves or others, is our saving grace. Nothing else and no one but God redeems us from absurdity and opens us to perpetual peace.

We will see that death and dying (and the "little deaths" as well) are very important experiences. The meaning of death in relation to spiritual development and the meaning of dying as part of living are crucial concerns not only in the elder years, but also throughout adulthood. Actually, a creative acceptance of our own immortality evokes a transcendent appreciation of life and fosters joyful living.

Throughout this book, the recurrent sign of contradiction will emerge. We must be willing to die in order to live. Such is the destiny of pilgrims who seek the Promised Land.

Chapter 2

A Vision of Spiritual Development

This chapter offers a vision—a way of looking at life—that sheds light on the problems, challenges, and possibilities of adult pilgrims who journey through deserts on their way to promised lands. The primary method is phenomenological insofar as it suspends theories, beliefs, and assumptions in order to explicate the meaning of experience. The goal is to describe and discuss spiritual components and dynamics of adult development.

Our theory of spiritual development is partly organismic in that it proposes that the span of life consists of developmental transitions, that one stage of development builds on what has gone before and leads to what is to follow. Such an epigenetic principle posits that our existence incorporates times when we are pressured to reflect on and perhaps restructure our lives. Transitions also occur because of personality and environmental factors. Throughout our lives, we undergo experiences that precipitate significant changes. And how we manage each transition primarily depends on many idiosyncratic and cultural factors. In short, our approach is contextually rooted in both nature and nurture.

Our vision is very important because it coconstitutes our meaning of reality and our consequent decisions and behaviors. Thus, our way of construing desert experiences is crucial in helping ourselves and others. Coping strategies and spiritual exercises are usually very helpful, but our way of seeing and being in the desert is paramount. Let us reenter the desert to look at how we see spiritual development.

DESERTS

Transitions begin with a movement from one phase of development to another, and the initial change can be seen as the threshold of a desert experience. It is a time when we can begin to see the desert's vast nothingness, hear its silent voices, feel its phantom touch, and smell its subtle aroma. It can both frighten and entice. It can be an opportunity or a danger. We can enter it cautiously, reluctantly, expectantly, or stop journeying and pretend the desert is not there. The time for a new season emerges.

Deserts are spiritual crises. Crisis, coming from the Greek *krinein,* to decide, indicates a significant time or turning point in one's life. Think of a crisis as an experience that occurs when we are thrown significantly off balance by an unexpected and acutely stressful event or developmental transition. Unlike ongoing stress, crises have a time frame. They may last for minutes, hours, days, months, or years, but they *do* end sooner or later.

When we are in crisis, we often feel a loss of control and power over ourselves and the course of our lives. We feel powerless, less power than we normally have, over the radical changes that are thrust upon us. We feel a sense of "dis" (negation, separated from, deprived of)—disequilibrium, disorientation, disruption, dislocated, disenchantment, distraught, disturbed, disgruntled, dismissed, dismayed, discontent, disarmed, disappointed, disengaged, disillusioned, dispirited, dissatisfied, and disconnected.

A crisis can be seen as potentially harmful and/or as an opportunity for growth. There are many kinds of crises, such as medical, psychological, traumatic, career, and developmental. Spiritual crises are always opportunities for growth. It is a time when "dis" is positive.

Desert, which comes from the Latin *serere,* to join together, and *de,* away from, refers to the time when things that are normally together come apart. Things that made sense are now in question. In the desert, we may feel abandoned—deserted. No-thing seems to make sense. Something or someone is radically missing. We may feel lost and be at a loss. We have lost our grip on things and are left with nothing to grasp.

When the ground of our being is shaken, we feel anxious and helpless. Our vulnerability, mortality, and ultimate dependency are acutely felt. Feeling that relying primarily on our own powers is simply inadequate, we come to admit that we are powerless—that we cannot save ourselves. We feel stripped of our normal supports, and we yearn for a more powerful and caring reality that will help us make sense of life and move on.

Not infrequently, God feels absent precisely when we need God present. We may feel alone and abandoned in the desert, reaching out to no one. Like Job, we cry out and ask why, what, and how. But no one seems to answer. Recoiling in anguish and often anger, we dread the prospect of a lonely passion. Consciously or unconsciously, we ask God or some higher reality to take this Gethsemane away, but our pleas feel unheard.

To follow God's way, especially when feeling abandoned, is countercultural. To accept our desert journey as a necessary avenue to experience God's saving and joyful presence conflicts with society's ethic of immediate gratification. To experience God's saving presence, in God's apparent absence, is nonsense to conventional wisdom. We will explore how we can come to this different approach in living—to no longer futilely try to save ourselves from oblivion. We can learn to leap in faith beyond our limited selves and lay hold of the unlimited resources of God's spirit. We can say, "Not me, but we, oh Lord."

Nevertheless, when we feel that our world is coming apart, we can be tempted to look for some magical miracle to save us. Drugs, sexuality, hyperactivity, or excessive passivity are common means to avoid the pain of self-discovery and spiritual growth. Actually, such well-intentioned attempts to find permanent peace and meaning are subtle counterfeits of the real thing.

How we manage these changes can vary considerably. For instance, radical changes usually evoke anxiety that can lead to denial, anger, or escape. With anxious fascination and openness, we can look for new growth. Persons who trust and accept their feelings will have an easier and more meaningful experience than persons who distrust and repress their feelings. Although deserts are universal opportunities, every individual has a unique way of responding to them. Our spirituality, especially its desert form, is significantly influenced by our physical, psychological, and social condition. We have indicated that while in a desert we can feel depressed and lost; however, deserts can become familiar and welcome places where in silence we hear more and in darkness we expand our vision.

Our thesis is that the desert purifies and empties us so that we can become more intimate with God, self, and others—we can be in the Promised Land. Our individuality, self-sufficiency, self-control, self-esteem—ourselves—are deflated so that we may be inflated in community and in God, in ourselves, and in others. We become truly ourselves through being with others. Being fundamentally on our own simply does not work. The mantra is "not me, but we."

Whether we like it or not, and despite being culturally unpopular, the journey through the desert is necessary to reach the promised land. But, desert demons entice us to seek power, pleasure, or self-idolatry as ways to escape our helplessness, pain, and dependency. False promises seduce us. Rather than trusting God or our Higher Power, we depend on ourselves. In this way, we provide the equation for our undoing.

Metaphorically, we feel more secure when we have a four-wheel-drive vehicle with plenty of gas and supplies, along with a map. But spiritual desert journeys have no map and material supplies, and our souls are the main vehicle of transportation. Indeed, there are supplies, but of a different order than material ones. When we enter the journey and travel for awhile, it can be awfully tempting to return to slavery. Or we may pitch tents in the desert, build idols, and try to have a perpetual orgy. Actually, nothing works except patient and persevering journeying through the desert until we reach the promised land. Although we can consult with veteran desert explorers to learn how to prepare for and make desert journeys, we are called to make the journey alone. And, in the midst of the desert, we come to be more with God.

DESERTS AS CREATIVE SUFFERING

Both pleasant and painful experiences are needed for spiritual development; one without the other leads to serious problems. To be sure, not all growth involves suffering. Experiences of love, creative play, and joyful times of celebration are some of the many ways to grow comfortably and with exhilaration. Such pleasant experiences are usually welcomed and are just as necessary as the unpleasant ones. The painful ones, however, usually cause more difficulty.

One way to look at pain is as a function of change, specifically of existing structures. Physiologically, a broken arm, colitis, and pancreatic cancer are definite changes in physical structures that cause pain. Psychologically, betrayal, contempt, and shame have painful consequences. Spiritually, the absence of serenity, feeling abandoned by God, and being lost in nothingness are painful. Pain demands to be heard. It pressures us to listen to and attend to ourselves. Heeding the message of pain not only increases our chances of survival but also helps us to heal and become better persons.

Usually, we automatically judge pain to be indicative of something negative, wrong, or unhealthy—and, pain often does indicate the change of a structure that is neither congruent with and supportive of growth nor in service of integration. For example, the pain of cancer points to pathological processes that destroy the organism. Psychologically, when we deny important experiences, we pay a painful price. To live without purpose and meaning is hell. Such pain—physical, psychological, or spiritual—conveys that something is awry, that care is needed.

Pain can also be symptomatic of healthiness. Healthy pain is construed as creative destruction in the service of positive growth and integration. For example, the pain of exercise and diet are in the service of health. Consider a man who adjusts to repressing hostile feelings. His awareness can be an uncomfortable movement toward learning effective ways to cope with hostility. Or, integrating new experiences such as assertiveness, love, and self-knowledge can be painful. Once again, pain calls for care.

In calling for care, pain is a force that unites us. Pain pleads for relief, for an adequate response from self and others as well as beyond one another to God. Pain encourages us to reach out for help, to let ourselves be touched. Pain is a universal equalizer; it is our common ground that binds us together. In pain, our existence is affirmed as coexistence.

And yet, paradoxically, pain wants to be left alone. For example, when sick, we want to be treated and cared for, but within boundaries. We want only so much interpersonal presence; then we want to be by ourselves. Besides calling out to others, pain also throws us back on ourselves. It invites us to become more aware of ourselves and to take better care of ourselves, thereby leading to more strength, freedom, and serenity as well as compassion. In this sense, pain is a gift.

A special domain of spiritual pain is the desert. Its pain pressures us to stop and listen to ourselves. Desert pain is seldom a message for prevention or treatment, but it is an invitation to live more fully. Our pain challenges us to become stronger through responding appropriately to our weakness. Rather than avoiding our pain, we accept it. Such acceptance is neither masochistic, whereby we get pleasure from suffering, nor does it reinforce or condone the pain. Paradoxically, our graceful and often ambivalent acceptance decreases our pain.

To interpret the pain of desert nothingness as positive rather than negative is a different approach. Many of us find it difficult to suffer in positive, productive, and meaningful ways because we usually judge pain as something to purge or tolerate. Unfortunately, common avoidance also eliminates possibilities of growth. Since the desert is an essential life force, an escape from its pain is an escape from oneself.

To further compound matters, many (if not most) models of mental health exclude the spiritual dimension. Some explain it as an illusion, a rationalization, or as unnecessary. Within such frameworks, the pain of spiritual development makes no sense. Construing pain as symptomatic of only physical and psychological processes, spiritual experiences are then distorted by reducing them to physiological and psychosocial interpretations. My contention is that spiritual experiences are real, essential, and paramount to being. To know desert pain and how to suffer it creatively is what this book is about.

How we suffer our pain is critical to growth. The etymology of suffering—the Latin *sub* (under) and *ferre* (to bear)—can help us to understand the necessity and positive value of suffering. How we bear or carry life's burden, demands, and pain highly influences the kind of life we live. To suffer life effectively and honorably engenders strong character that enables us to manage well and to live in serenity. A life without suffering is bland, shallow, and boring. Without suffering, the most important experiences would not exist.

PROMISED LANDS

In time, we settle down and live according to the values learned in the desert or those which resulted from a denial of the desert. The way we live depends highly upon our experience and lived remembrance of the desert. In contrast to desert times, this process of implementation is relatively stable and secure. We emerge from being pulled apart in the desert to come together with ourselves and others in a land of promise. We come from creative chaos to creative order. Our suffering leads to joy.

Now the accent is on presence more than absence, serenity rather than restlessness, and sense instead of nonsense. The fruits of the Holy Spirit console and secure us. Our being is lighter. We are inclined to dance and sing—to celebrate being spiritual. We want to proclaim the good news that God is with and in us. We enjoy being a sanctuary and ambassador of God's love.

Being careful to avoid complacence and being vigilant in nurturing ourselves, we can live more easily and celebrate being in the Promised Land. We find ourselves in the midst of spring enjoying life's emergence. We anticipate the restful and rejuvenating days of summer as well as the splendor and climax of the fall. It is a time of light and warmth, planting and growth, rest and recreation.

Our experience of "dis" (disconnection, disconsolation) recedes. We feel more comfortably connected with others, God, and ourselves, and consequently feel consoled. The ground of our journey feels solid, our direction is clearer, and our purpose motivates us. We are *personae viator*, persons on the way—to the Promised Land.

Actually, the promised lands are more on the order of oases. The Promised Land toward which we continually journey is actually the place where and the time when we will experience permanent harmony and fulfillment. It is the kingdom of God. Meanwhile, we are on earth, not in heaven. To reemphasize: We are never completely fulfilled, happy, at peace, or without suffering and unrest. We never get "it." We are always getting it. Since we are growing in fulfillment, happiness, and peace, there are always times of unfulfillment, unhappiness, and discontent.

We are pilgrims who build the kingdom on earth, moving closer to the Promised Land. On earth, we get tastes of heaven and hell. Our journey through deserts and promised lands leads to our destiny—the Promised Land. Our vocation is to live the good life until we come to death—the final desert leading to the ultimate Promised Land.

Thus, adult development—physically, psychosocially, and spiritually—is an ongoing process of transition and implementation, of restructuring and structuring, of dying and living. We move from a relatively stable and familiar land into an upsetting and foreign desert, where we confront radical and critical issues. If we emerge from the desert in a healthy way, we come to a more stable, stronger, freer, more serene, and virtuous way of living. To be sure, however, the heart is always restless until it rests with God.

TIME

Time and its relation to life and death can be helpful in understanding our approach to spiritual development. We use two meanings of time: *chronos* and *kairos*. *Chronos* refers to quantifiable "clock time." Technically, it corresponds to the modern notion of time as a series of isolated moments and it lends itself to being measured and used. If we live only according to chronological time, we futilely strive to live for the present as if our past and future were not at stake. We live frantically as if there is no tomorrow and no life after death—as if life stops evolving. Viewing development only from a chronological point of view tends to be static, impedes a dynamic vision of aging, and engenders a weary and depressing outlook.

Kairos refers to "sacred time," to occasions when the regularity of our chronological time breaks down, allowing more significant and transcendent experiences to break over us. Kairotic time is qualitative and gratuitous, rather than quantitative and controlled. It is a sacred time, an opportune time, a time that embraces and transcends all seasons and ages. It is a time for holy presence.

Both modes of time are necessary and desirable. One without the other makes for less than healthy living. A scheduled time of *chronos* is needed for functional order and productivity. If we did not use and follow chronological time, life would be unproductive and chaotic. We can also use *chronos* to service and foster the more important and life-giving times of *kairos*. We can use our time and space to increase the likelihood of experiencing those kairotic times that make significant and lasting differences in our life. For example, although we cannot guarantee a vacation to be enjoyable and significant, we can take the chronological time to have a vacation that may result in *chronos* and its consequences. *Kairotic* times, such as significantly joyous and sad times, are beyond our control. Although we cannot cause them to happen, we can increase their likelihood. Without times of *kairos,* life becomes insipid and tends to lack purpose and meaning.

Sacred events experienced in *kairos* redeem us from the boredom of our daily grind. Inspired by the Holy Spirit, our everyday chronological lives become enthusiastic, our psychosocial functioning becomes easier, and our service to self and others becomes more productive and meaningful. In fact, our entire lives improve when we experience the saving spirit in *kairos.*

Spiritual deserts as well as promised lands are rich in the possibilities of *kairotic* events that break over us. Such events may pressure us to reevaluate our use of all time in order to be more open and responsive to spiritual living. Or these times may invite us to take stock of life, to ask the classical questions of why am I here, where am I going, and what is it all about? Does God exist? Is there a God who cares for me? Why live? The desert questions our reason for being.

Listen to Charles Cummings: "In the desert experience of God's absence we can meet him in hidden forms; His desert presence and transforming power are concealed by a cloud that only a vision of faith and love can penetrate . . . the desert experience is our spiritual purification for a new life of freedom and love in the land that God will show us" (Cummings, 1978, pp. 22-23).

The desert experience is a sacred and decisive time that results in progress, fixation, or regression. It is a time of opportunity when we come to a crossroad and can move deeper into or farther from authentic living. We can face reality and, through some pain, become more mature, happier, and more enthusiastic. Or we can run from reality, benumb our sensitivity, and repress the radical questions that call for crucial responses.

Such turning points can occur at any time. Times that are unique to the individual may evoke a desert. Death of a beloved, marital crisis, trauma such as rape or assault, physical or mental illness, or economic disaster may throw us into a desert. These idiosyncratic deserts (as contrasted with life cycle ones) force us to deal with not only the catastrophic event, but also with other issues that emerge from it. For instance, a beloved's death pressures us to reflect on our own death and life, on how and why we are living/dying.

Along with idiosyncratic events, deserts are also a function of our dynamic nature. We are emergent beings who are called to unfold, to explore, and to settle—to restructure and structure, to differentiate and integrate. The archetype of polar opposites incorporates the rhythms of consolation/desolation, light/darkness, being/nothingness, pain/pleasure, deserts/promised lands. Life itself, at various times, invites us to enter the desert.

In any case, we neither create nor control the desert; rather, the desert is a graced time beyond our control. And yet, paradoxically, this powerless time leads to more power and control. Hopefully, we are willing and able to accept God's desert invitation. Sometimes, we may be willing but unable due to fatigue, sickness, or environmental responsibilities. Then we can postpone the journey until we are ready. Or we may be ready but unwilling, opting to stay where we are or to circumvent the desert with pleasure or power. In time, the desert will break our will. But give thanks, for such a breakdown can be a grace to a breakthrough.

In kairotic, desert times, the meaning of life is put to question. We are thrown back on ourselves and asked to take stock. We find ourselves on center stage, with only ourselves to face, and classical questions emerge. Who am I? Where am I going? Whence do I come? Death, God, faith, hope, love, work, play, sex, suffering—life—are brought into question. Coming face to face with the essential meaning of life is a spiritual issue of major magnitude. To know and live our true reason for being is a matter of life and death.

IS A STAGE APPROACH VALID?

Considerable debate exists, among psychologists who study adulthood, concerning whether or not predictable adult transitions actually occur. Some researchers contend that life cycle stages do not occur, that adult development is stable and consistent. Others say that significant changes may occur, but they are idiosyncratic and occur at nonspecific times. A third group proposes that transitions occur at fairly predictable times.

Our model represents an attempt to respond to and integrate various differential models. For instance, deserts may occur in certain age ranges, and they may occur because of one's life experience, age cohort, personality, fortuitous factors, and so on. And it is possible for both the existential and idiosyncratic to occur simultaneously. Indeed, whatever generalizations we may draw about adults, not all people necessarily grow in a rhythmic way. Still, many do—and all of us grow spiritually in a dialectic way.

Most spiritual writers contend that we must go through deserts or times of desolation and darkness. Although these crises are seldom linked to specific developmental stages, a recurrent theme is that spiritual growth is impossible without desert-like experiences. Being enlightened includes purgative dark nights, feeling consolation makes no sense without humbling desolation, living in faith presupposes creative doubt, promised lands are surrounded by life-giving deserts, and life is permeated with death. From this perspective, critical times are essential components of the spiritual life.

A relatively well-known model that posits physical, psychosocial, and spiritual crises as necessary for growth is the twelve-step program of recovery. Arguably, this approach is the most dominant and effective approach toward recovery, particularly for addicts and codependents. Pertinent to our concerns is that twelve-step ways of living are wholistic and primarily spiritual. In contrast to a treatment approach, a twelve-step recovery model focuses on growth and development. It is particularly congruent with our paradigm.

Its first step is to admit that we are powerless over the problem—addiction, codependence, physical or mental illness, life/death—and that life has become unmanageable. Alcoholics Anonymous, the foundation and framework for all twelve-step programs, holds that the experience of powerlessness and unmanageability (which constitute a crisis) is essential in coming to sobriety or health. Twelve-step programs posit that only a Higher Power (a reality greater than the individual self), often called God, can lead us to sanity. Out of powerlessness and unmanageability, we can come to give our lives and wills over to the care of God as we understand God. Without such a breakdown, a breakthrough is practically impossible. These initial three steps resonate with our model of the desert experience.

Furthermore, the middle (action) steps involve a process of taking stock of one's life. With the help of a Higher Power (God, fellowship, sponsor, etc.), recovering persons are encouraged to take a moral inventory, to share it with God, the self, and another person, to ask God to remove their defects of character, and to make appropriate amends. Indeed, these steps speak of the radical questions and responses that are part of desert conversion.

The final three steps, which suggest ways to maintain and foster spiritual growth, are congruent with the more settled times of the promised land. But any twelve-step program emphasizes that all the steps must be continually practiced, for the desert is always potentially present as are temptations to escape it via behavior such as addiction or codependence. In short, admitting our powerlessness (desert) leads to a Higher Power who enables us to live better lives (promised land).

Not just addiction and codependence, but almost any radical change in life can throw us into a desert. For example, a woman may experience spiritual depression and loneliness when her husband dies. She yearns for the presence of her husband, is depressed by his absence, is thrown back on herself, and in a certain sense is asked to start a new life. In her depression and loneliness, she begins to reevaluate her life and to come to a deeper appreciation of life. Through the death of her husband and her own dying, she comes to see life anew. As another example, if a man in his fifties is suddenly fired from his job, he may be thrown into a desert. The loss of his job throws him back on himself and pressures him to take stock of himself. He is not only forced to find a new job but, more important, he may have to make significant changes in his lifestyle.

Special situations, such as psychotherapy, may induce desert experiences. The therapeutic atmosphere can encourage us to go beyond our normal way of looking at life and sometimes engender a desert journey. The acceptance, understanding, and concern of the therapist help us find the courage and acceptance to confront ourselves in and out of the desert.

Solitude and meditation also increase the likelihood of desert experiences. In meditative solitude, we do not rationally control or will a desert experience, but we set conditions that are conducive to its emergence. The serene and simple situation of solitude and the mindless mindfulness of meditation lend themselves to desert reflections much more than everyday, task-oriented situations.

Another way to experience the desert is at certain times throughout life. There are no exact ages when everyone enters the desert, but there are general periods when many of us are more likely to experience a developmental crisis. And indeed, we experience these developmental deserts in unique ways. The proposed stages of development are flexible and have a wide range with regard to age. The older we get, the more variables there are, so it is impossible to predict with certainty. Thus, our framework is more of a guideline to what often occurs.

It is unlikely for anyone to undergo a severe crisis in every adult stage of development. Nevertheless, most of us do experience at least one significant transition in our lifetime. And such crises may be due to idiosyncratic events or existential (epigenetic) dynamics, or both. Furthermore, crises can vary in intensity from very mild to severe. Our contention is simply that aging is a significant factor in development.

For instance, although "midlife crisis" is probably an overused and perhaps trite phrase, many people do experience a transitional time in their early forties. Many midlifers do reflect on their limits and mortality, their past dreams and future goals, their relationships, androgyny, and themselves. Many midlifers, more because of age than situational events, begin an inner journey that differs from their previous outer journey.

Age ranges or stages are given to concretize the theory as well as to enable us to compare ourselves with one another and to prepare for our own desert experiences, whether or not they fall within a time frame. Even though epigenetic transitions do not follow a strict chronological schedule, many people do experience significant changes within or close to the age parameters. These ranges are not indicative of how long the transitions last for every individual, for there is considerable variability from person to person.

Such existential deserts are important if for no other reason than that they tend to keep us honest. For example, if we are running away from ourselves or living unhealthy lives, the emergence of desert nothingness pressures us to reevaluate and renew ourselves. In spite of being highly conditioned by our environment and culture, we are not totally programmed by them. Our nature, along with nurture, forms our development.

Since it is our contention that spiritual growth is primarily progressive, all times build on and influence one another. For instance, fixation at one time of development will influence subsequent times; a particular difficulty at one time in life may engender regression to a more comfortable time. On the other hand, healthy acceptance of difficult times facilitates acceptance and growth at other times and often makes future desert journeys easier. Desert crises are not necessarily excruciating, but they are critical in the sense of fostering or impeding growth. It is rare to live a holy life without difficult times. A key to healthy and holy growth is to accept and manage our difficult times—to face the present in faith and love, to look to the future in trust and hope, and to celebrate the past in gratitude and praise.

Chapter 3

Desert Life

We have listened to some desert stories and have offered a model of spiritual development. Our next project is to present succinct analyses of the desert's structure and dynamics that are significant to spiritual development. Keep in mind that the desert is a metaphor used to point to certain transformative experiences. Other similar and often interchangeable terms that indicate the same kind of experiences include dark night, desolation, purgation, nothingness, doubt, and crisis.

In our approach, experiences of nothingness are especially related to desert experiences. Both are metaphors that point to the same experience. Desert connotes a time (*kairos*) when and a place where significant meaning in our lives is questioned, challenged to change, and summoned to restructure. "Nothingness" connotes a subjective condition of being when nothing makes sense. Nothingness occurs in the desert and the desert incorporates nothingness. Both renew, restructure, and reform.

BEING IN THE DESERT

From our beginning, we are given certain parents, family, values and expectations, socioeconomic standards and possibilities, and, in general, guides for living. The environment in which we find ourselves significantly influences the way we experience reality. As children, we discover that some people are more loving and trustworthy than others and that Mommy and Daddy are, for better and/or worse, indispensable. We come to value some things more than others. Perhaps money is paramount in one family while books are in another. We also learn that certain behaviors, feelings, and thoughts bring rewards while others evoke punishment. What happens in desert experiences is that we no longer take our ways of making sense for granted and we radically question what we have assimilated. We experience life differently, no longer being content as we may have been. The desert is a rupture in conventional living.

Normally, things seem to come together and work out. Everything seems to have some connection to something else, and life more or less makes some sense. In the desert, we find ourselves no longer connected to things, people, self, and God the way we once were. In such a turmoil of disconnection, everything seems to break down and "no-thing" seems to work. Life seems more disordered than ordered, more disintegrated than integrated, more dark than light. People, things, events, values, thoughts, and feelings change and no longer make the same sense as before. Life may seem so different that we wonder if anything really makes lasting and significant sense. Nothingness permeates us.

No longer do we have the security of the past; our dependable world of meaning is no longer certain. We may doubt whether anything will ever make sense again and, at times, we may feel helpless in trying to cope with this erasure of meaning. Everything seems uncertain and nothing gives us support. And our heaviness and struggle are painful reminders of the relative lightness and ease of the past.

We may feel deserted—left with only ourselves in this dry and barren land. We often experience people more present in their absence than in their presence. Although we desire to make genuine contact with others, we feel powerless and hesitant to try. In the desert, people remain distant as "other." Everything and everyone seems to recede into the background of life, leaving oneself in the foreground. We stand starkly before ourselves. We alone must face, direct, and affirm ourselves.

We usually experience loneliness, yearning for the understanding presence of another. People who were once familiar may feel different and distant. Parents seem to be in a different world and suddenly friends seem unavailable. People in general are "out there," and God is absent in presence. Nobody is there for us.

In the desert, we also feel alone. Although we may or may not miss and yearn for the presence of others, we feel that we are an island separated from the mainland. Being by ourselves, we are thrust into nothingness, alone with nothing to grasp. There is nothing to distract us; we stand purely before ourselves and perhaps before our hidden God.

Desert people frequently experience the darkness and heaviness of depression. We feel tired, weak, and helpless in trying to make sense of things. Feeling stuck, it is difficult to move, to get motivated, and to be involved. And to move toward what? Purpose, direction, and people are somewhere lost in darkness. We seem to have lost our grasp on things. Vision is clouded; nothing seems clear anymore. It seems that life is pointless and has little value or positive effect. Nothing has importance and nothing makes its impact. Feeling leveled, we wonder if we can stand up to make sense of things. Our existence is felt as resistance. Are we adequate to the task of integrating all this nonsense?

Although we often feel anxious, there is nothing much we can put our fingers on. We are anxious about nothing in particular and everything in general. The past is beyond our grasp, the future seems unattainable, and our present seems to be a quagmire of nonsense. We are no longer back there, nor are we quite out there. We are anxious about being nowhere, and we may dread falling into a bottomless, black pit. Who am I? Where am I going? What will happen to me? What is going on? These are the unsettling questions that engender angst.

In the desert of nothingness, we can be afraid of losing our grip and way. The desert demons of our dark side may petrify us. We may be afraid to look at life's shadows and may be tempted to run from the desert to the slavery of repression and addictive behaviors. We may be afraid that God is an illusion and that religion is the opium of the people. We can be afraid of the dark, of the devil, of sin, and of death. Yet, in fear and trembling, we can come to a reverent awe.

A vague and sometimes strong sense of guilt may permeate our existence. Not being able to pinpoint what we are guilty about, we nevertheless feel a strange incompleteness and a basic indebtedness. Although we do not feel all bad, we do not feel all right. Why should we feel guilty when we have done nothing wrong? Closely related to this existential guilt is existential shame. Rather than feeling guilty for doing something wrong, we feel that our being is wrong. We feel less worthy than we once thought. Standing in nothingness, we may feel that we have deserted ourselves. We feel seen as painfully diminished. We may even wonder if anyone, including God, could love us.

The desert can engender boredom—a feeling of being stuck in what makes little sense. Nothing gives us satisfaction, nothing offers success; nothing evokes lasting fulfillment. Everything seems to lack genuine excitement and solid sense. We may get tired of being bored and our tired feelings make us more bored.

Frustration also shackles us and weighs us down. Frustration is not about this or that, but about everything in general. Nothing seems to work out. Our good intentions and efforts seem to fall short. Will anything make sense? Frustration can weigh heavily and wear us down.

Sometimes we get angry. We have had it. "Why me?" we may ask. "What sense does this make? Will it ever end?" Building a slush fund of anger, we may find ourselves resenting seemingly peaceful people. We may blame and resent God for deserting us, for leaving us with nothing. We may get tired of trying and being angry, and slide into apathy, making us indifferent, and "out of it." We no longer seem to care. Nothing turns us on.

In the throes of the desert, we may feel anguish. We feel as if we are drowning in nonsense and nothing can save us. We want to leave our weary and aching bodies in a place of peace. Is there a way to peace? Crying out in the desert seems to evoke no response. No one seems to respond to our silent shouts.

We cannot emphasize enough that the desert experience is positive. Although in the throes of nothingness we may experience little sense, our absence of meaning is a quest for transformative meaning. Our apparent loss of meaning is actually an active quest for relatedness and fulfillment. Our yearning in loneliness is a search for the intimacy of love; our desolation in aloneness is a springboard to the togetherness of love. Our emptiness in depression is a quest for the fulfillment of joy. Our change in anxiety calls for the strength of courage; our groundlessness in dread is a preparation for the solidarity of trust. Our burden of guilt is a summons for the lightness of integrity; our walls of shame are a cry for the liberation of love. Our shackles of frustration are a plea for the liberation of autonomy; our heat in anger is a purgation for the coolness of serenity. Our lethargy in boredom is a thirst for the vitality of enthusiasm; our lifelessness in apathy is a retreat for the reentry into life. Our pain in anguish is a breakdown for the breakthrough of consoling serenity; our nothingness in death is the passage into eternal life.

THE DESERT AS A FUNDAMENTAL LIFE FORCE

We are born with dynamics that motivate us to survive and encourage us to grow. One life force is to maintain ourselves. A natural propensity to preserve and to protect ourselves is manifested in satisfying basic needs such as hunger, sleep, and adequate shelter as well as protecting ourselves from harmful activities; otherwise, we would die. Adequate love and care are equally necessary for survival; otherwise, we would feel psychologically and spiritually dead. We also maintain ourselves by preventing illness and unnecessary discomfort. We learn that the pain of sickness and injury is a message to avoid destruction and to heal.

Furthermore, we are urged to explore and discover reality, to learn from it, and to use and enjoy it. Children take initiative in their curiosity and play, and older children become industrious in their drive to discover more of reality. Adolescents seek to solidify their identity as well as expand their interpersonal and personal experiences. Likewise, mature adults have a natural inclination to think and feel about things, generate ideas and actions, and to promote a sense of wonder and contemplation. We have a natural propensity to differentiate reality, especially ourselves. Thus, the life force of differentiation makes for change: extra- and intrapsychic change.

Along with differentiation is the propensity to integrate, which literally means to make whole. Seeking solidarity and wholeness, we desire to bring new experiences together. Especially when we have extraordinary experiences, such as falling in love, feeling hurt, or being anxious, we want to get "it" together and to feel at home with ourselves. In short, life involves the perpetual processes of differentiation and integration.

Any of these life forces can be overemphasized or even become pathological. If we invest too much time and energy in maintaining ourselves, we become too comfortable and content and we fail to mature. Holding on exclusively to what we have, we fixate to avoid discovering new ways. On the other hand, when we stress differentiation, we try to be open to everything and become addicts of change. Our relative lack of integration leaves us diffused and shaky. We become hysterical liberals who change everything in contrast to compulsive conservatives who maintain everything.

The desert is an existential life force that moves us to seek spiritual truth and intimacy. It is an epigenetic force that motivates us to grow until we die. The desert is more subtle than other life forces; its necessity and meaning are not as apparent. In fact, it is often seen as negative and contrary to life instead of as a necessary way to grow spiritually. The paradoxical truth is that the spiritual loneliness, depression, and anxiety experienced in the desert are opportunities for spiritual growth.

For instance, loneliness may be construed as a lack of involvement and therefore a deprivation of life. Desert loneliness, however, means that we have had contact with people and desire deeper involvement with them; our loneliness is a desire to be intimate with others and with God. And, when we impede our journey through, or escape from, the desert, life forces us into such loneliness. We frustrate our development.

Desert depression, unlike clinical depression, is not simply a negative loss, a helpless heaviness, or a blind introspection. Such spiritual depression can be an appeal to look more deeply, an opportunity to listen more carefully, and an impetus to live life more fully. The loss and helplessness of depression can lead to significant gain and freedom. The depression of the desert can lead to the joy of the promised land. Likewise, anxiety is often seen as indicative of conflict or as a symptom that one is being closed to oneself. Although this is one form of anxiety, desert anxiety can mean that we are in a time of transition. In a sense, we are nowhere, but on our way. Such anxiety can mean that we are searching for more significant meaning and have not yet found it. Spiritual anxiety leads to a deeper and stronger self-identity that goes beyond itself to being connected to others and God.

A main reason for entering the desert is to discover deeper and lasting meaning, direction, and purpose through an apparent lack of meaning, direction, and purpose. That is, the yearning in loneliness, the loss in depression, the uncertainty of anxiety are ways of enriching one's life. The barren absence of the desert leads to the rich presence of the Promised Land.

The "breakdown" of a person's worlds of meaning can actually be a "breakthrough" to more authentic meaning. In the desert, we can experience a creative destruction of the illusions of living. We question cultural values, standards for acceptable behavior, goals of a successful life, our identity, our reason for being, and the sense of it all. We are urged to confront and renew our lives. We are invited to rekindle life's basic questions and come to better answers. What is the meaning of freedom, serenity, commitment, compassion, forgiveness, and love? Where and how can we realize them? Where, how, and why are we going to live? Such desert experiences must be accepted and nurtured for, without experiencing *nothing,* we cannot find *something* lasting. We can only reach the Promised Land through the desert.

While wandering in the desert we usually encounter our limits, weakness, and powerlessness. Sometimes, we may feel too weak to go on—weary of struggling. We realize we have much less power over life than we assumed, and this awareness may scare us to death. We are pressured to humbly acknowledge that even our control of ourselves and of what we own is limited, that ultimately we are powerless. And yet, our desert journeys can lead us to promised lands where our limits lead to the unlimited, our weakness engenders strength, and our powerlessness evokes new power.

Our dark side demands recognition. Our primitive desires, instinctual urges and rages, and our capabilities to do evil confront us. This shadow of existence begs for recognition, understanding, and integration. It forces us to humbly admit that life is not so simple and nice as we once assumed or wished. Evil, complexity, turbulence, and chaos all want their places in the house of humanity. It is tempting and common to avoid, repress, or numb the darker side of life, and therefore violate life and weaken ourselves. Avoiding darkness keeps us in the dark. The desert invites us to face these demons, understand them, and learn to transform them into positive activities. Once again, good without evil, simplicity without complexity, contentment without turbulence, order without chaos, and light without darkness are illusions.

God seems to hide or even disappear in the desert. Even if we have had a lifelong relationship with God, God's absence may be intensely felt. Where is God? Why is God no longer here for me? Is there really a God? Why/What is God? What difference would/does God make? What is happening? Why?

We can get confused, frustrated, and angry about this rupture in our spiritual lives, especially if we have centered our lives around and in God. Feeling that we are being treated unfairly, we may get angry at God, become cynical toward religion, and doubt the existence of God. Why would God do this to me? I tried to live a good life and to follow God's ways. In the name of God, I struggled and sacrificed. Maybe God is an illusion.

People who have not lived an overtly spiritual life may also find themselves in this desert of divinity. Even though the existence of God has not been a relevant issue, they begin to experience the absence of God, and this peculiar absence of presence haunts them. They feel pressured to consider the possibility of a divine reality and what difference such a presence would make. And what difference does the absence of God make? They can no longer be content to act as if there is no God. Maybe a reality that is greater than themselves can make a significant and perhaps ultimate difference.

Whoever we are and from wherever we come, when we are in the desert, the ultimate reason for living becomes an issue. And, God cannot be divorced from such an existential quest. In fact, God is at the base of our questioning. God challenges and gently mocks our certainty. In experiencing our limits and powerlessness, we come to experience the Unlimited and All Powerful. Being humbled helps us to let go of our control and to let God comfort, console, enlighten, and guide us.

So, desert experiences are important, if for no other reason than that they keep us honest. The desert beckons us to enter its land, to explore its landscape, to listen to its sounds, to see its beauty, to feel its climate, and to touch its life. Its demons relentlessly challenge us and its angels perpetually help us. These desert hounds of heaven keep us restless and restive. Because of deserts, we are always searching for, wondering about, and discovering new horizons. Being in the desert keeps us alive—always journeying to the Promised Land.

Chapter 4

Desert Languages

Deserts speak in many languages. Unlike our conventional verbal language, their messages are primarily nonverbal, ambiguous, and often ambivalent, and their communication is more affectively spiritual than cognitive. Desert truth is mysterious, paradoxical, and transcendent. Common words are spoken in uncommon ways, including loneliness, aloneness, depression, anxiety, fear, guilt, shame, frustration, anger, boredom, apathy, and anguish. The proposal is that these affective expressions of spirituality invite us to explore and progress through the nothingness of deserts to enter into promised lands.

The purpose of this chapter is to explore the similarities and differences between psychological and spiritual affectivity. For example, we will reflect on the spiritual meaning of loneliness as well as psychological forms of loneliness. Thus, two basic kinds of experience are explored: spiritual and psychological. Although distinct from each other, these feelings are interwoven. The contention is that we often assume that all feelings are physical and/or psychological (and indeed many of them are), but we neglect to listen to spiritual feelings that "speak" to us and orient us differently than psychological ones.

Spiritual affective expressions can be called existential in that they are necessary and essential for holy and healthy living. In our model, existential means that we must undergo these experiences of desert nothingness in order to grow spiritually. Our choice lies in the way we face them. For instance, we must experience spiritual depression periodically throughout our lives, but how we experience it depends basically on us. We can repress, escape, numb, or accept our depression. Rejection impedes growth and acceptance opens up opportunities for positive change.

Our psychological life is more idiosyncratic than existential. Psychological feelings are unique to each individual and, unlike existential experiences, they are not epigenetic or essential for healthy living. They may or may not happen. For example, we may experience idiosyncratic loneliness when a loved one is absent, but if he or she is present, we are not lonely.

A main difference between spiritual existential and psychological idiosyncratic experiences is that a spiritual experience is rooted in a person's personality structure as an essential life force, while a psychological experience is contingent on a person's unique personality and situation. Spiritual experiences are necessary for authentic living, but psychological ones can promote or impede health. Existential anxiety, for example, occurs because of our nature, or existence. On the other hand, idiosyncratic anxiety may arise because of a stressful situation or because of repressed feelings. Such psychological stress and repression are a function of the individual's coping style. To be sure, how we cope with our psychological life impacts our spiritual life.

Our primary point is that deserts of nothingness and their languages are existential experiences. To be human is to experience nothingness. Consequently, this archetype of nothingness must be accepted and managed effectively to achieve healthiness. Instead of avoiding, purging, or violating ourselves, we can learn to face, foster, and help ourselves. Depending on our attitudes and approaches, we can run from ourselves, or we can encounter and become more of ourselves.

Learning desert languages opens up new worlds of meaning. Construing our uncomfortable feelings differently evokes new ways of responding to our unsettled selves. These healing ways need not be in opposition to medical and psychological treatment models, but rather can complement them. Once again, remember that the way we view ourselves and others highly influences the way we respond, which significantly impacts our well-being.

LONELINESS

I feel like I'm on the outside looking in. I see people and I want to be with them, but I can't find a way in. I try, but I end

> up empty. I think how good it would be to be close to someone, and if only someone would understand. What a difference that would make—for someone to really care for me and for me to care for. Will I ever stop feeling so lonely?

As this woman indicates, loneliness involves a yearning to be with, yet a frustrated movement toward others. We try to reach out to people, but our reach falls short. Although we desire to be with people, we feel as though we are on the periphery of their presence. We want to touch and to be touched, but our struggle feels fruitless.

Lonely persons feel the presence of other people more in their absence than in their presence. To "feel the absence" of others means that we once had some meaningful contact with others, but no longer have it; otherwise, we could not "miss" them. Contrary to our desires, they are not there for us.

Consider the experience of this man:

> I really felt lonely one night after work. Everything was quiet, snow was on the ground, and a full moon was out. The quietness almost spoke. It was like I felt myself by myself. I looked and no one was around. I felt a yearning to be close to someone, and no one was there. It was so empty. Yes, I wanted to be with Joan. I really miss her. It hurts. I tried hard to have things work out, but they didn't. I don't know what to do. I tried, but . . . I still want to be with her, but it looks like it's not going to happen.

Although lonely persons feel cut off from human relations, particularly close relationships, their separation is not complete. Feeling lonely does not mean that we feel completely by ourselves, absolutely isolated in a humanless, vacuous existence. More likely we feel that we are neither really involved nor absolutely noninvolved. We struggle, yearn, and search for contact. Lonely people suffer the painful presence of others not being with and for them. And it hurts to feel that no one stands by, for, and with us. Loneliness is frustrated love—love from afar.

Life makes less sense when loneliness pervades us. Behavior lacks purpose and direction when it is not related in some way to others. As one said:

> It makes little sense to work just for myself. I get tired of going to work—work for what? When you're lonely, nothing seems worthwhile.

A lonely existence is painful because it tends to be meaningless. Lonely people repeatedly ask themselves: "What do I have to live for? Who really cares?"

Psychological Loneliness

From a psychological perspective, loneliness can have many meanings, which vary from healthy to unhealthy. One type of unhealthy loneliness is based on fear. The closer such lonely persons get to others, the more anxious they become, often because they have been hurt in intimacy. Past overtures toward intimacy may have been rejected, ridiculed, or ignored. These lonely people find themselves in the quagmire of being afraid of the very thing they want and need most. They yearn for intimacy and yet they are scared to death of it.

Unhealthy loneliness may be symptomatic of dependence. Dependent persons feel an urgent need for other people to give them life. They need others to satisfy their needs for comfort and security and, when someone is not nurturing them, they feel intensely and anxiously lonely. Since their worth depends on others, the absence of others evokes anxious loneliness as well as desperation.

Although dependent persons are willing to do almost anything as long as people are nice to them, unconsciously they are compelled to suck the life out of people. Of course, people soon withdraw from them. As a client said:

> I can't understand it. I try to do everything I can for people. I try to be nice. But no matter what, they eventually withdraw from me and I'm left by myself. I guess I do get mad, but it hurts. What should I do? How can I make someone love me?

Loneliness can also be healthy. For example, when lovers are separated from each other, they miss each other, but their temporary loneliness can help them to appreciate and be more sensitive to each other when they meet again. Consider when someone close to us dies. We intensely feel our loved one's presence in absence. Paradoxically, loneliness is natural and healthy when we keep the dead or missing ones alive in our appreciation and gratitude for them.

Spiritual Loneliness

In the desert of nothingness, we often experience spiritual loneliness. We yearn for intimate contact with another person and we feel the other person more in absence than in presence. At times, we are thrown back on ourselves and we feel estranged from people in general, and somewhat distant from those who are close to us. Such desert loneliness encourages us to reevaluate our feelings about and attitudes toward love and intimacy. We question our relationships with our friends and people in general.

In the desert, we are given the opportunity in loneliness to deepen and broaden our identity. We come to realize that self-discovery is a necessary prelude for self-surrender and that loneliness is an excellent preparation for intimacy. We not only become concerned with self, but also with our relationships with others. Without loneliness, we would lose our connection with others, both living and dead. Loneliness proclaims a life of being with others. When we grow in and through loneliness, we are unlikely to exploit, manipulate, or play games with others, for we have learned to respect and love others.

Spiritual loneliness invites us to question ourselves in relation to others. It pressures us to find our place with others. Such existential loneliness evokes questions such as the following: Who am I going to love? How am I going to give myself to others? Where can I find someone to commit to? What is the meaning of love? Paradoxically, through their apparent absence, people can become more present. The loneliness of desert nothingness is an appeal to be with and for others, to be a better person for others. Loneliness beckons us to be a person for others. It behooves us to accept, listen to, and respond to a call.

Desert loneliness is a fulfilling process. It is not a loneliness that is empty and futile like some forms of unhealthy loneliness. It motivates us to share ourselves and to give unconditionally. When we realize that the important issue is not just me or you, but us, we go beyond our individual needs to appreciate the needs of others.

Our spiritual loneliness tells us that we are called to love one another, to build community, and to surpass ourselves in love. In the desert of loneliness, we can hear the call to love one another—and being together in love is the promised land.

Most important, spiritual loneliness is the prelude to intimacy with God. We eventually learn that no person, except God, can adequately respond to our yearning hearts and that only God can be there for us unconditionally—all the time, no matter what. Regardless of our state of being—saint-sinner, up-down, worthy-unworthy, present-absent, positive-negative—in the desert-promised land, God is there for us. The challenging difficulty of desert loneliness is that God is often present in absence. Our challenge is to be patient with faith and hope to wait until God eventually appears, more clearly, from the cloud of unknowing.

Why does God become more absent than present? We have seen that absence is a yearning that can deepen our presence to another and that loneliness is necessary to grow in intimacy. Paradoxically, God's absence is, in some respects, a fuller presence because God's presence in absence goes beyond our intellectual understanding and calls for faith—an acceptance of experiences that we cannot explain. When God moves beyond our grasp, God may be present more fully. In sacred time *(kairos),* God's presence in the dark night leads to enlightenment. The cloud of unknowing leads to more knowledge; our experience of being abandoned leads to greater intimacy. Such is the process on earth. Heaven is when there are no dark nights, clouds of unknowing, and feelings of loneliness and abandonment.

Our spiritual loneliness tells us that only God is an adequate response to our transcendent yearning. No human being can permanently fill our hearts. As adults, to need love from a particular human being (including spouse and friends) is dysfunctional. As children we *do* need love from our parents, but as adults our well-being cannot depend on the love of another human being. When we take such a codependent approach, we empower the other person; in a sense, we make the other person our God. When another human being becomes our primary source of consolation, guidance, and salvation, we displace God. Consequently, we become frustrated, angry, and depressed because no human being can always be there for us unconditionally.

Indeed, we need love to survive and thrive spiritually. While needing love from a particular person does not work, we do need love for and from others (rather than a particular person), and for and from God and self as well. The sustaining source of this communal love is God. In spiritual loneliness we come to appreciate that God is the only particular person who can always be there for us. And God's perpetual presence helps us to accept and manage when particular persons are unfair, mean, or simply unavailable. Although we can learn these truths at any time, the desert is a special opportunity to come to such divine intimacy.

Desert loneliness leads to divine dependency. In spiritual loneliness, we realize our need to give our will and life over to the care of God. Our restless and fearful yearning is ameliorated when we can surrender to God. However, to be able to let go and be suspended in nothingness can be frightening. What if no one comes to me? What if there is no God? What if I remain in this empty darkness?

We need faith and hope to be willing to wait for the opportune time to leap into what/who is beyond and includes our individuality. Our challenge is to let go of our ego control, simply be, and allow God to love us. Our Holy Spirit—the uncreated energies of evolving Love—evokes and responds to our desire to be in communion. Being the Source of Love, God consoles and heals our broken hearts. Ultimately, we rest and celebrate in God and one another.

ALONENESS

Aloneness and loneliness can be confused, for they are similar and different. We are alone when we are by ourselves and, unlike loneliness, we do not necessarily yearn for contact or feel the pain of not being with another person. We can be alone and not lonely.

In being alone, we feel our singularity and uniqueness. Other persons are not the main issue for us, but the focus is on "me." A woman expressed herself this way:

> It wasn't like my first separation from my boyfriend. Then, I hurt and really missed and wanted to be with him. This time

> was different. I felt all by myself and, although it wasn't painful, it wasn't painless either. I really didn't think about being with him; instead, I felt an intense awareness of me. I realized that my life was in my hands—that it was up to me to live my life. Funny—although it was a little scary, I felt strangely strong.

Aloneness can be physical or psychological, or both. We can withdraw from people so that we are physically by ourselves but psychologically *with* people—that is, not psychologically alone. On the other hand, while in a crowd, we can feel alone. And we can be both physically and psychologically alone.

Another possibility is to feel psychologically alone and lonely. A thirty-five-year-old woman expressed her aloneness in this dream:

> I felt like I was the only person on earth. It seemed like everything lost its gravitational hold and was flying off the earth—everything except me. I felt the world was turning into a vast desert with me in the middle of it.

This woman felt that she was totally by herself, feeling intensely her individuality and separateness. She also felt lonely in her aloneness; she painfully missed and yearned for personal contact.

Psychological Aloneness

Like most experiences, aloneness, physical and psychological, can be healthy or unhealthy. Unhealthy psychological aloneness is a painful experience. To feel completely by oneself can mean being cut off from any hope of contact. This type of psychological aloneness is often unhealthy because one feels unworthy of being with another person and it may lead to despair—no hope for contact. Since lonely persons are still yearning for contact, they are more hopeful.

Physical aloneness can also be less than healthy, as when we avoid or withdraw because of unrealistic fears. Physical aloneness may be a refusal or an inability to accept the responsibilities of being oneself with others. For instance, some people withdraw psychologically and physically because they are afraid of being hurt or embarrassed by others. Psychologically, when we withdraw from facing unpleasant aspects of ourselves or others, we have little opportunity for coping well. We build a wall to protect our frightened and vulnerable selves. And our withdrawal becomes a prison of aloneness.

A less than healthy form of psychological aloneness occurs when we withdraw from our nothingness. For various reasons, we refuse to accept our desert experiences and consequently become more out-of-touch with ourselves. The paradox is that the more we run from the desert, the more we become alienated and less able to communicate effectively with others. Withdrawal from the desert leads to slavery.

It is foolish to expose ourselves to unnecessary hurt; we can face what is going on and then, if necessary, choose to withdraw in a healthy way. It is appropriate and healthy to detach with love (of self and other) when attacked with hostile criticism, amiable manipulation, or cold indifference. Healthy aloneness presupposes a healthy affirmation of reality, and unhealthy aloneness is a fundamental negation of reality.

Healthy aloneness helps us grow in responsibility and freedom. It is often appropriate to exit a situation to be alone to think, rest, and re-collect ourselves. The most important form of such aloneness is solitude—when we choose to be alone physically for healthy reasons, such as study, thinking, enjoyment, listening, self-exploration, meditation, recollection, contemplation, or just being.

The silence and serenity of solitude are conducive to being. In solitude, we are less polluted and distracted by noise, busyness, and thinking, and we are more apt to be open. Solitude is basically a nonthinking time when we take a creative pause to listen, to re-collect, and to go deeper into life. In solitude, we can be purely present to, listen to, and ponder our experiences, and thereby deepen our encounter with self and others. The zenith of solitude is contemplation—a pure communion with reality.

Spiritual Aloneness

Solitude particularly lends itself to desert encounters. Although we cannot will such an experience, solitude makes it more likely to occur. In solitude, we may be tempted to escape from or purge the discomfort of nothingness. Hopefully, we are graced with the courage to listen to the absence of reality and the wisdom to know that this peculiar absence is a form of presence that leads to a higher degree of fulfillment. Both the comfortable experiences of promised lands and the uncomfortable experiences of deserts are important ways of growing in solitude.

In desert aloneness, we feel that we are at center stage and the spotlight is on us. But no one is around: "I, myself" am the audience, actor, writer, director, and producer. The show is about and for me.

We experience ourselves as being "the only one in the world"; our own existence is intensely felt. We strongly feel our unique individuality. We know that no one can stand exactly where we stand or see exactly how we see. Being alone is a stark reality. The absence of interaction with others can enable us to listen more clearly and to focus more intensely on our own experience. And, in such aloneness, we are invited to renew ourselves for being with and for others.

We can feel a sad sense of joy in realizing that we are always, in some way, alone. Even though we may be deeply in love, we know that we cannot be with our beloved constantly and absolutely. There are moments when we, alone, must face reality. And yet, we can be glad because our aloneness is an opportunity and impetus to discover ourselves in order to give ourselves. We come to realize that our aloneness is in service of love.

We may feel that God has deserted us, leaving us alone to fend for ourselves. Along with everyone else, God does not seem to be around for us, yet, when we listen to the silence, we begin to hear new sounds. A new language is spoken and a new communication occurs. God speaks with different words and is manifested in absence. Indeed, we are renewed by God's adumbrated presence. Our challenge is to be patient and strong, and to stay with God's absence/presence. In time, God will appear more clearly and intimately. Spiritual solitude is an opportune time and place to encounter God directly. In solitude, we can listen to God's word without distraction, see God's vision more clearly, and touch God's presence more closely. God and I can come face-to-face without intermediaries. No one or no-thing is between us.

Thus, especially in the aloneness of solitude, we can experience God directly or indirectly, overtly or covertly. These polar opposite ways of experiencing God are necessary to grow spiritually. When

God is absent, we are called to have faith, that is, to accept the incomprehensible, and to believe that we are coming closer to God. And when God is present, we are called to be humble and grateful. We must trust this divine process.

DEPRESSION

Usually, we hear and think about depression in its clinical forms, those that indicate pathology and dysfunction. However, similar to loneliness and aloneness, there are different forms and meanings of depression. We will first investigate factors that are common to depression and then explore the two basic forms of depression: idiosyncratic/psychological and existential/spiritual.

In depression, we find ourselves dejected, tired, unhappy, listless, and sad. Life feels heavy, gloomy, uneventful, and dark. We are "depressed" or "pushed in"; it is as if the air is pressed out of us. We seem to be swimming upstream. Since motivation and interest are low, we are likely to withdraw. Pleasure, enjoyment, and fun are absent or overwhelming chores. We feel down in the dumps and may feel helpless and hopeless. Sometimes, we may feel so empty and worthless that suicide feels like the most meaningful act.

Having a low self-regard and judging ourselves in terms of limits, we are likely to dislike, criticize, and blame ourselves to an extreme degree. In short, our hyper-introspective vision fixates on the negative, impeding us from seeing much positive outside and within ourselves.

Key dynamics of depression are often some form of loss and helplessness. Our loss may be the loss of something, whether it be a person, something of value, an experience, serotonin, or anything significant. When we lose someone or something that is valuable to us, we feel more or less depressed, as though parts of ourselves are missing. And feeling relatively helpless to improve our well-being, we feel trapped in a deep, dark pit.

Psychological Depression

Depression is caused primarily by an internal loss (endogenous) or by an external loss (exogenous). Some researchers think that depression, especially the endogenous type, is due primarily to biological factors. For example, change or loss of neurotransmitters (such as serotonin) or menopausal hormonal changes may cause depression and thus may be treated pharmacologically. Internal losses can also be psychological. For example, if a perfectionistic person fails, he or she "loses" self-esteem and may feel depressed. Repressed anger can also result in depression. Depression can also occur in response to an external loss. For example, the sudden loss of a loved one radically changes our usual way of living. We mourn our loss and hopefully come to accept our loss. We may feel depressed when we lose some "thing" that has personal meaning. An investor whose paramount value is money may become suicidally depressed when the stock market crashes.

Unhealthy depression impedes functioning and healthy growth. Such depressed persons feel trapped and constantly tired. Vital functions are usually impaired—there may be too much or too little sleeping and eating. Severely depressed people become totally immobilized, feeling so shackled in depression that they cannot act at all.

Healthy depression is an appropriate response to a situation, external or internal, that eventually helps us to mature. We can become legitimately depressed when we fail to acquire a needed job; however, this depression is temporary and manageable. We try to learn from and be strengthened by the depressing situation. Death of a significant person engenders a difficult and healthy depression. For example, when a woman is depressed over the death of her husband, she may become relatively disoriented and immobilized, but eventually she comes to a deeper appreciation of life perhaps in and through her spouse's death.

Spiritual Depression

Metaphorically, people who experience spiritual depression are "de-pressed" or "pushed in" so that the focus of attention is on the self. We are asked to stop being so busy, to slow down, and to take time out for ourselves. Spiritual depression pressures us to look again at life and to take stock of ourselves. As an adult man said:

> Depression doesn't have to be "so bad." I think it can be "so good." Sometimes, I'll even listen to music that usually makes me depressed. But I enjoy it. Like when I listen to the *Patheti-*

> *que,* I descend into life's sadness and darkness, and I become sad and dark. And yet, I feel more real and in touch with life. Paradoxically, my deflation leads to inflation. Although it's not the only way of seeing things, I see life differently through my depressed eyes. I become more sensitive, compassionate, and strong. I slow down to look deeper into life.

Unlike psychological depression, we do not experience a loss of this or that, but rather we feel depressed about nothing in particular. Suddenly, those things and people we value and have relied on most of our life seem to lose meaning. We feel radically lost in nothingness and we feel at a loss for words to explain our seemingly sudden change of behavior. We lose the familiar sense of things around us; our world and people seem out there and foreign. People are different, values change, and our past world is suddenly outdated. In a sense, we lose our old grip on things.

Life becomes heavy. No longer do we feel light and playful. In the throes of such depression, we feel that life is only a burdensome struggle and we wonder if we will ever feel comfortable with anything. Nothing seems to make sense. We have nothing to hold on to and nothing to believe in.

The meaning of spiritual depression is that we have nothing to lean on and nothing to stand on, except ourselves and God. Our depression in nothingness throws us back on ourselves and asks us to find our place and pace in the world, to search for something we cannot lose, and to find meaning that is part of our being and that no one can take from us. In looking down and within, we are encouraged to look up and out. To believe, especially when God is absent, serves to strengthen us.

Desert depression affirms the limits of living. Can we begin to accept and see the possibilities of our limits? Can we love all of a person including his or her limits? Can we love another because of his or her limits, not only in spite of them? Can we find the wisdom to avoid being seduced by limits and consequently be blind to possibilities? Can we find the discipline to actualize ourselves within our limits and, consequently, be free persons? When we experience a loss of fundamental meaning, we are motivated to renew ourselves and to find deeper meaning in life. Our depressed eyes enable us to look for and to discover new horizons of meaning that embrace, make sense of, and transcend our limits. In time, we come to a deeper awareness of the Unlimited.

Our depression also encourages us to be more sensitive to and compassionate with others. When others are depressed, we are unlikely to judge their experience as necessarily negative, but more likely to accept and to listen to its meaning. Instead of "fixing" them with chemical and psychological treatment, we can help them journey through their dark night.

Our emptiness cries for fulfillment and our limits thirst for the Unlimited. When we can journey through this desert of depression, we come to a more comfortable and joyful land. We come out of the dark pit to an enlightened land. The absence of meaning *does* lead to deeper meaning. The breaking of dawn *does* usher in the sun. With the help of God and others, we travel with courage through this valley of death.

It is good to know that God journeys with us in the desert. Although we may feel we have lost God, God is in the shadow of our being. When we emerge from the desert, it is as if we can see again and God is out of the shadows. In the desert, God helps us to accept and manage our loss as well as making a promise to fill the hole in our soul. To pray, not to get rid of, but to move through the depression, is wise and helpful.

With grace, it is also helpful to "move" physically, psychosocially, and spiritually. Avoid getting stuck or becoming depressed about being depressed. Walking, talking, listening, praying, and other healthy movements are effective ways to manage and grow from spiritual depression. With the help of God, ourselves, and others, we can move through and out of the desert of depression to a lighter land.

ANXIETY

As anxious persons we feel tense and tight, uncertain and uneasy, as if we are trying to walk on quicksand. Instead of feeling at home with ourselves, we feel disharmony, out of sorts, ill at ease, and at odds with ourselves. We feel that something is bothering us, as if we are unable to handle an impending and unknown danger. We feel pressured to change or do something, while feeling uncertain of how or even of our ability to respond. Control is tenuous and threatens to break down. Frequently, anxiety also indicates that our identity is changing or threatens to change.

Perfectionistic persons, for example, may feel anxious when they cannot control a situation. Since their sense of worth depends on perfect control and performance, their identity is threatened. Furthermore, if they doubt their ability to cope with a stressful situation, they may withdraw in a panic state. People who experience forbidden feelings become anxious, for their feelings threaten their identity and/or engender feelings of helplessness. People often feel anxious when they fall in love because they feel pressured to change and explore new possibilities.

Psychological Anxiety

Psychological anxiety often occurs as a response to environmental stress. When we begin a new job, we are usually more or less anxious about not knowing where we stand. We cannot know exactly how to or if we can meet the employer's expectations. Furthermore, the new job may offer us a change that may make a significant impact on our lives, but what kind of change and impact remains unanswered. The healthiness or unhealthiness of anxiety depends primarily on whether anxiety mobilizes effective behavior, or whether anxiety impedes us or is the result of negative coping.

Unhealthy anxiety is often due to repression. Denial of important experiences because of unrealistic standards evokes anxiety. Some standards force us to reject feelings that demand expression and, in our attempt to cope with this untenable conflict, we feel anxious. For example, if we cannot admit to feeling angry, we will use considerable time and energy to prevent any angry expression. When anger is provoked, we become anxious and may even panic, or we manifest symptoms such as rigidity and avoidance that serve to control our anxiety as well as forbidden angry feelings. Our anxiety, overt or covert, is a message that we are being closed to our angry self rather than being open to and learning from our angry feelings.

Some neurotic people are anxious most of the time. They feel threatened by and inadequate to deal with almost any kind of stress, whether the source is primarily inside or outside themselves. Other neurotic people live constantly in conflict between feeling one way and thinking the opposite way. Although they control their anxiety, they waste a great deal of time and energy that could be invested in more productive and fulfilling experiences. Although their defense mechanisms are strong, they are too weak to face and resolve their conflicts.

Anxiety can also be an integral part of a growth experience. For instance, persons who experience a sunset aesthetically may undergo some anxiety along with joy. They feel drawn to a new and deeper world of experience that eventually leads to a higher degree of personal integration. Their happy anxiety is in service of growth and, although they are clearly uncertain, they welcome the invitation to move beyond the ordinary.

Anxiety is a way of telling ourselves and others that a significant change and a challenge are occurring. Whether positive or negative, healthy or nonhealthy, anxiety should be listened to because it is a way of understanding oneself. Healthy anxiety proclaims that we are growing in new ways and unhealthy anxiety beckons us to listen to how and why we are fighting ourselves.

Spiritual Anxiety

Descriptions of spiritual anxiety are not uncommon in the writings of struggling saints. Particularly in their dark nights and times of desolation, anxiety is a common visitor. In these deserts, we feel the ground of our existence being undermined. We may experience ourselves in free flight, not knowing how we fell off the cliff and not knowing if we will land safely.

Although we may have felt secure, we find the meaning of our lives giving way. Being left in the middle of nothing, we feel uncertain about everything. We are no longer in the familiar past and yet not in the future, leaving us in a situation of "not-yetness." And if we feel urged to make sense of our anxiety, we feel even more anxious, for we comprehend nothing.

Actually, anxiety means that we are on the way to a deeper mode of living. Our anxiety moves us to ask questions that call for lasting answers. We search for a meaningful place that cannot be taken away.

Dread can be considered a form of spiritual anxiety wherein we find ourselves in the throes of nothingness. Existential dread calls us back to our roots, inviting us to wonder about the possibility of any behavior whatsoever. Paradoxically, when we confront the possibility of nonbeing, we come to a fuller appreciation of being. In dread we question again: What makes me be? Why am I? Where am I going? What ought I do? Can I make it? Can life really make sense? Why should I live? Feeling lost and swallowed in the vortex of nothingness, we feel called to seek our place and to live at our pace.

The dread of being lost in the desert encourages us to gain an appreciation of the fullness of living. Anxiously standing on the precarious ground of nothingness, we actually prepare ourselves to be with and for others more solidly and harmoniously. Dreading no-thing and every-thing humbles and weakens us. Feeling so lowly and earthly, we look up for a higher presence. In reverent awe we begin to get a glimpse of a God who can restore our strength and peace. We can offer our dreadful selves to this saving Presence. Being humbled in dread can prepare us to be redeemed and reconciled. Out of weakness, we come to greater strength.

With God or a Higher Power/Caregiver, we become stronger and more serene. Bonding our dreadful selves with God eventually ameliorates our anxieties and fears and enables us to think and act more effectively. Still, since we are on earth, we are never completely healed nor do we achieve perpetual peace. Thus, we are always more or less anxious and that is one of the reasons there is a loving God.

FEAR

Perfect love casts out fear. But perfect love among humans rarely exists for very long on earth. Perfect love is more a description of heaven. And, indeed, on earth we at times *(kairos)* taste the delights of heaven. We are called to perfect our love and to accept God's perfect love—to build God's kingdom. Such strengthening love, along with other virtues and coping strategies, gives us the courage to circumvent and ameliorate fears and, at times, purge them.

Fear is a warning of danger that someone, something, or some event can harm us. Most basically, fear alarms us to fight or flight and, more rationally, to have other options as well. Fear cautions us and it can help us to protect ourselves. Fear affirms and protects our vulnerability.

In contrast to anxiety, fear is usually a response to a particular person, place, or event. Anxiety is more general and free-floating, whereas fear is usually specific and concrete. Since we are fearful of something, we can often articulate and manage fear.

Psychological Fear

Fear can be a healthy response to real dangers, or it can be an unhealthy response to unrealistic, imaginary, or transferred dangers. Rather than helping us, unhealthy fear impedes and can paralyze us. For example, obsessive-compulsive fears are unrealistic and severely diminish our freedom. Phobias or irrational fears motivate us to avoid situations or leave us to be overwhelmed by them.

We can also have fears that were appropriate in childhood but are inappropriate in adulthood. Ridiculing, rejecting, angry, and mean people probably scared us as children. They had the power to put fear in us. Our challenge is to work through such childhood fears so that they are not transferred to and do not interfere with our adult lives. Unlike childhood, we now have choices to cope effectively with such difficult people. Instead of shrinking in fear, we can keep an adult stand.

Healthy fear is an appropriate response to what can harm us. Such fear can mobilize our defenses to protect ourselves. Out of fear, we can learn to set boundaries that maintain our safety and allow for successful management. Instead of being paralyzed by fear, we listen to what we are afraid of and think of ways to handle what threatens our well-being.

Spiritual Fear

From a spiritual perspective, fear points to a different reality than psychological fear. Fearing nothing rather than something is difficult to grasp. When nothing makes sense, we can fear the possibility of life remaining relatively meaningless. We can be afraid that we will not be able to manage a life without purpose. Our fearful selves may need the security of knowing what is happening and how life will turn out. We may be afraid of getting lost in the desert of nothingness, or that life is really nothing and everything is an illusion.

We may be afraid that the spiritual life and its theological explanations are fictions used to allay our insecurities. We may be afraid that we are pursuing something that does not exist. "What if all this spiritual stuff is a sham?" is a fearful thought. We may be afraid of discovering that there is no God. More important, we may be afraid to address such questions and pursue the truth.

What if we discover that there *is* a God? Knowing there is a spiritual life that includes God, a knowing that comes from struggle, makes a significant difference. Our whole lives can be changed and that can be a frightening realization. We can run from the desert because of what we may learn and how it will affect our lives. Addictions, in particular, numb our fears and put us in temporary euphoria.

We can fear facing our dark sides, to confront our demons—those negative forces that pull us down to less than we can be. To be aware of our potential for evil can engender fear and trembling. To descend into the underworld takes courage in response to fear. Actually, to be unafraid would be foolish. To realize that we are accountable for what we do and how we live can put the fear of God in us. To know that we are not in complete control of our lives and that, ultimately, we are powerless can also be frightening. We have plenty to be afraid of.

To face our fears with love for and from God, ourselves, and others may not dispel fear, but can certainly diminish it. Courage—love facing fear—helps us to manage fears rather than being controlled or overwhelmed by them. Actually, when we face and manage our fears, we become stronger. Paradoxically, our fears can strengthen us.

SHAME

Although guilt and shame can be similar and are often interrelated, they are distinct. Guilt centers on something we do or feel that we have done, while shame is more a matter of "being." In shame, our feelings can run the gamut from feeling less worthwhile to feeling utterly worthless. The accent is on "being diminished."

Since we want to avoid being seen, we may hide our true selves behind masks of security and competence or of detachment and apathy. We avoid being seen as worthless, for being seen increases our shame. In shame, we want to disappear.

Psychological Shame

Unhealthy shame is due to factors such as deep inferiority, basic distrust and worthlessness, feelings of being wrong or being a mistake, and feeling essentially stained. Obsessive-compulsive people, for example, often harbor unconscious feelings of shame that lie beneath their obsessive thoughts and compulsive acts. It is as if their suffering souls futilely try to be perfect because they feel so utterly imperfect. They try to be spotlessly clean because deep within themselves they feel dirty. Somehow, they try to get everything just right because they feel so wrong. Instead of accepting and loving themselves as they are, they feel compelled to perfect themselves to be accepted and loved. They cannot really accept the fact that love is for imperfect and stained people. On earth, love is meaningless without imperfection, for love desires to perfect imperfection.

Consider victims of sexual abuse, particularly repeated incestual acts, who feel deep shame. They feel so stained that they cannot be seen or really touched. They feel unworthy of what they need most—healthy love. "Who would love such a despicable person? Who wants used and broken goods? Who wants a reject?" are some of their cries. They hide and are imprisoned behind the walls of shame. Inside they feel ugly, unacceptable, untouchable, and frightened to death. To be seen is fatal.

Unlike the victim, perpetrators of sexual abuse should feel shame. Not only have they severely harmed others, but they also have violated themselves. To doubt their worth and feel loneliness may be the beginning of recovery. To be shameless could be sociopathic or at least repressed. Shame can be a perpetrator's saving grace.

Spiritual Shame

We are good, beautiful, and joyful people—and we are bad, ugly, and sad people. Because we are born imperfectly on earth and not in heaven, we are shameful people. We are not completely formed, worthy, and trustworthy, but we are existentially incomplete, deformed, and unworthy as well. Being fallen people, we need redemption. Shame means that we are on earth and not in paradise.

The desert, in its purity and solitude, helps us to face our shameful selves. Silencing demons of judgment or ridicule, we can begin to look at our dark side, our vulnerable neediness, and our sinfulness. When we can accept our diminishment, we can begin to grow stronger and more worthy. Out of shame, we can become strong enough to be seen as worthy of love.

Although we may know that God's loving eyes are always on us, we may feel ashamed of God's long, loving look. We want to avoid God's gaze. Our heads turn down and inward, away from God. We feel too unworthy to let God embrace us. Being seen, we feel, diminishes us and is awfully painful. Yet when we get down on our knees, we can begin to look up for redemption.

God enables some people to accept and love our shameful selves even when we hide them. Their accepting our nonacceptance may enable us to show parts of our shameful selves, to be seen, touched, and reconciled. Since a violation of trust and love puts us in shame, only unconditional, trustworthy love will melt the walls of shame and redeem us.

Spiritual shame affirms our need for God and others. In shame, we encounter desert darkness and a descent in our lives that call for redeeming acts of unconditional love. Since we are not self-sufficient, but rather integral members of a community, isolation from community is damnation that exacerbates our shame.

Our challenge is to let ourselves be seen in our unworthiness, in our sins, and in our nothingness. Like prodigal offspring, we are embraced as we are—in our filth, in our fall from grace, and in our brokenness. God's and people's love reconcile us to them. Our shame has brought us back home—being together with others in love.

GUILT

Although guilt can be considered a type of moral anxiety, we will look at guilt as similar to, but distinct from, anxiety. Guilt usually emerges when we act in a way that is contrary to certain standards.

Generally, we feel uneasy, low, and heavy for doing something that we feel is wrong. We feel bad because we are not doing what is expected of us, what we should do, or what we ought to do. Trustworthy persons do not feel good when they break a promise; puritanical persons feel bad when they have sexual fantasies; and, loving persons feel guilty when they manipulate others.

We can feel guilty because we feel we broke a rule, either an internal or an external one. Young children, for example, may feel guilty when they are caught rummaging through a closet that is off-limits. Older children feel guilt when they hit a sibling even though they are not caught. They no longer need their parents to punish them, for they have internalized the parents and consequently they punish themselves. Children basically operate according to a "should" and "should not" framework that brings reward and punishment. Thus, they abstain from certain actions to avoid punishment.

Mature adults do not feel guilty because they transgress a standard or because of a fear of punishment, but because their behavior is wrong. For example, when they lie, they do not feel guilty because they broke a commandment, but because they harmed others. Their guilt comes from a conviction to care rather than from fear.

Psychological Guilt

Unhealthy guilt usually indicates that we have unrealistic standards and values that impede or deny important experiences. For instance, perfectionistic persons who feel good only when they do something completely right, feel guilty for almost any kind of imperfection. Persons who have rigid standards against any feeling of aggression will feel guilty when they feel hostile. In fact, for them, the feeling is almost the same as the act. Thus, when they begin to feel hostile, they immediately repress their feelings so they can live up to their standards of being a nonhostile person. To compound matters, such persons seldom know why they feel guilty.

Adults who behave according to a child's system of guilt are, at best, immature. Since these persons abstain from certain behavior because of their fear of external or internal punishment, their "good" behavior is actually centered on themselves. They confess primarily to relieve their guilt—only to feel better, not because they hurt another person. Instead of involving creative restitution, their penance is basically self-centered.

Healthy guilt is neither neurotic nor immature. When a healthy person exploits someone, guilt is the price for violating another's well-being. Loving persons feel guilty because they were unjustly angry, acted hostilely, or because they put themselves above someone else. Guilt tells us that we are doing harm and violating healthy living.

People with healthy guilt make creative restitution. They try to make up for the harm they have done to themselves or to others by doing something that not only compensates for, but also helps to improve the situation. For example, a husband who is guilty of overworking realizes that he is harming both himself and his family. He takes measures to work less and to use more time and energy to enjoy himself and his family. A daughter who is hostile toward her mother makes creative restitution not so much by apologizing, but more by improving her behavior. Both husband and daughter make amends.

Spiritual Guilt

Spiritual guilt is not due so much to bad behavior or to breaking standards. Paradoxically, such existential guilt comes more from nothing. In spiritual guilt, we become aware of a creatively restless mood residing in the core of our being—a guilt that judges us as imperfect. Such guilt challenges us to progress and improve. With spiritual guilt, we hear an inner voice that says go on, be better, realize your dreams, be more.

We feel guilty for not being more of what we can become. Especially in the throes of nothingness, we begin to experience how insignificant we really are in the light of history, humankind, and eternity. Would our deaths have any significance? Have we really left a meaningful impact on the world? What difference does it make that we live?

We may compare ourselves to others. We feel guilty not so much for what we have done but for what we have not done. Our guilt does not center on work accomplishments, monetary possessions, or social success; it is more a reflection of nonbeing. We ask ourselves how much we have really loved and have given ourselves to others, and we wonder how much we have really celebrated and enjoyed life. Our guilt is a summons to take stock of ourselves.

With desert guilt, we begin to realize how much we are indebted to humankind and that, without other people, especially our parents, mentors, and friends, we would neither be nor have the possibility of being who we are and doing what we do. We affirm radically that our life is a gift and that we are indebted to others for our lives. We feel guilty for owing so much to so many and knowing that we will never be able to pay off our debt, especially the debt of love.

Spiritual guilt reminds us that, fundamentally, we are no better than anyone else. Because of our guilt, we are less inclined to pull rank or to be violent and more inclined to be sensitive and compassionate. When we see our brothers and sisters being unjust to one another, we feel guilty and think, "There is one of our brothers or sisters, a member of the same human group, being violent." Although we feel guilty when anyone is evil, we do not bury our heads and do some meaningless penance; instead, we make creative restitution for our own evil acts and for the acts of others, primarily by living a good life.

Although we experience a basic uneasiness in recognizing what we are not, paradoxically, we begin to see what the fullness of being is. Original guilt is a radically positive experience that keeps us honest by putting pressure on us to live more fully and to give more lovingly. Spiritual persons always have horizons to see and possibilities to realize. Spiritual guilt fosters authentic pride and humility: an affirmation of who we are and are becoming—pilgrim people emerging out of nothingness into being, out of deserts into promised lands.

We feel guilty before God for our deliberate and nondeliberate sins—and we can feel guilty for nothing in particular. Our spiritual guilt points to our omissions of being. We can feel guilty for not being as close to God and others as we could be. We can be guilty for missing opportunities to celebrate God's presence. We can feel guilty for avoiding the nothingness of desert journeys. We can be guilty because our community of humankind is far from living in peace.

Such spiritual guilt is a function of who and what we are. It urges us to be true to our better nature and to be fully alive. Our consciences remind us when we stray from God's way, that is, when we fail to foster peace among all people. Spiritual guilt helps us to be and do good.

FRUSTRATION

Frustration usually means that we are thwarted in attaining what we want or need. We feel blocked and held back in reaching our goal, or we feel inadequate in not being able to achieve some end. We feel tied up and shackled in areas where we want to move. Part of us wants to move toward something or someone, but we find ourselves not being able to move successfully. We feel stuck.

Frustration can lead to other feelings. For example, frustrated persons may become depressed if their inability to achieve something results in a significant sense of loss. A person who needs and desires an increase in pay can become depressed when he or she does not get the raise.

Frustration can also lead to anger. Instead of being depressed, we may become aggressive and try to change the situation. Children may throw temper tantrums when they cannot immediately get what they want. And, some of us act as children in this same way. Or we try to make things happen and use force to achieve our goals.

Psychological Frustration

Psychological frustration occurs when we cannot satisfy needs or reach goals. When we cannot adequately satisfy our basic needs, we usually feel frustrated, depressed, or angry. Hungry persons are often tense and irritable, and tired persons are often jumpy and depressed. Poor persons who constantly see opulence may become frustrated, depressed, or angry.

External and internal forces can prevent us from reaching our goals. We may be blocked by factors outside our control or by our own inability or lack of motivation. A woman who aims to change her job conditions may be stopped by her boss. A man may talk a good line but may really be unwilling or unable to implement his ideas.

Unhealthy frustration can have many sources. Consider perfectionistic persons who frequently feel frustrated because they seldom reach their goal of perfection. People who have sexuality as their highest value and those who have social recognition as their ultimate concern are frequently frustrated because their satisfactions and achievements are inadequate and temporary. Persons who hold back certain kinds of emotional expression feel frustrated because they are not being what they can be—affectively effective. Harboring unrealistic expectations or hoping that someone will change are common and debilitating causes of frustration.

Learning acceptable and healthy modes of behavior often involves some frustration. For example, when a child learns to postpone immediate satisfaction, the consequent frustration can be in service of learning. The discipline of students, artists, and athletes also involves frustration, which is eventually in service of freedom and success.

Healthy frustration is not the result of repressed needs or unrealistic goals, but rather it is in service of growth and maturity. As mature adults, we know and accept that we do not always get what we want and that life can be unjust and absurd. When we accept that frustration is a part of life, depression and anger are ameliorated. We learn that frustration is part of the process of achieving success. For instance, suppression of immediate, short-term gratification (sex, drugs, anger) can be in service of long-term gains. Saying "no" (frustration) can be in service of a "yes" (growth).

Spiritual Frustration

In the desert of nothingness, life can be deeply frustrating. A twenty-year-old expressed herself in this way:

> Will it ever end? How long must I go on feeling this way? What can I do? Will I ever be able to do anything really meaningful? Nothing makes sense. I try, and try, and try, but things don't work out. I feel so frustrated.

Spiritual depression and loneliness lend themselves to frustration. When we feel turned in on ourselves and feel we have lost significant meaning, we feel frustrated. Striving to find our old solidarity and being unable to reach it leaves us frustrated. Our yearning in loneliness leaves us frustrated; our striving to make sense of people, things, and life may involve frustration; and our realization that *nothing* makes the *most* sense often leaves us immersed in frustration. What we want most—fundamental freedom and peace—we cannot get. We are frustrated with life.

Basically, we are always somewhat frustrated in never achieving perfection and in never becoming fulfilled. We can never be perfect lovers, workers, givers, receivers, celebrators, and mourners. In sacred times, we may have moments of perfection, but only for moments—just enough to nudge us to chase perfection. Spiritual frustration means that we are always struggling to perfect ourselves, that we are always *homines viator*, people on the way.

The "no" of nothingness is an appeal to seek a "yes." Our frustration urges us not to be content with life and not to be satisfied with normal things. We refuse to simply maintain ourselves or to overestimate the value of temporary satisfaction and success. Rather than simply holding on to the temporary, our restless spirits motivate us to seek permanence.

It is not uncommon to be frustrated with God, especially when we are lost in the desert. We may want and need God to help us escape the desert and settle in the promised land. But God does not seem to respond, at least the way we want. Perhaps we assume that since we have led a good life centered around God, life should be just to us or that we should be led out of the desert. We are frustrated and angry with God, for God does not seem to respond to our wishes. Why does God leave us in our misery? Where is God?

It is a mistake to assume that the desert is a bad place to be and that God is not with us. We can change our view of God and the desert and listen to the silent God who speaks to us through our spiritual feelings. Especially in the desert, we realize that nothing on earth is permanently fulfilling. Our frustration can help us to connect more with God and God can help us accept our frustration and, paradoxically, lead us to a less frustrating and freer life.

We must be patient. Instead of being frustrated with being frustrated, we can accept, hopefully with the support of others, reality as it is and not need it to change. In time, life unfolds and leads us to more life. Patience may feel slow and frustrating, but any other way is slower and more frustrating. Let go and let God. Such is the way of patience.

ANGER

Anger is an aggressive "no," a protest, and a heated dislike. Anger wants reality to be different than it is in order to meet our standards, expectations, or needs. In anger, we do not like what is happening, and we are urged to change it. A common goal of anger is to change someone or something via force.

Anger and associated feelings such as aggression, hostility, and rage may be the most problematic and challenging emotions. Seldom do we use these feelings to foster growth. Instead, our approach to anger more often leads to negative consequences such as alienation, fatigue, and more anger.

We get mad at ourselves and others for being mad. We regress, deny, project, rationalize, and displace our anger. We have not learned to accept, listen to, and benefit from our anger. Instead, we use negative defense mechanisms that only exacerbate our anger and its underlying feelings. Eventually, we act out impulsively or inappropriately.

We may take the opposite approach—blatant expression. When angry, we express it, assuming that such "honesty" is healthy and helpful. Recent research has shown that such angry ventilation or "letting it out" increases the anger, alienates others, and fails to resolve the problem.

If "open expression" and "closed repression" make matters worse, then what does help? Indeed, it is vital to express our feelings to ourselves but not necessarily to others. Acceptance and awareness of feelings enable us to listen to and learn from our feelings. Rather than repression, we admit to anger; rather than expressing our anger, we first claim it. Then, we can decide if it is appropriate or helpful to ourselves and others to express our anger. A wise approach is to "share and check"—to share anger and check to see how the other person responds. It may be appropriate to suppress our anger, that is, to affirm it and then put it aside for awhile. In any case, we need not follow a prescription of "all or nothing."

Anger has many motives. For example, we have seen that we can be angry because we are frustrated. Feeling so thwarted, we want to do something about it. Dislike and injustice often evoke anger. We may get angry when our routine is disturbed or because our expectations are not met. Controlling persons may get angry when things do not go their way. Parents may show either just or unjust anger when their children go beyond the limits of acceptable behavior. A boss may be angry when she discovers that her employees are malingering or are doing poor work.

Keep in mind the distinction between angry feelings and angry behavior; they are related but not the same. As stated previously, we ought to claim, name, and listen to our angry feelings, whether they are healthy or not, for they are important sources of truth. Anger, like all feelings, seldom lies. By learning what our angry feelings are trying to teach us, we can enable ourselves to take appropriate action.

Angry behavior is acting out angry feelings. When we fail to listen to the angry self (for whatever reasons), we are apt to "act out" our anger inappropriately. To identify feelings with behavior only causes unhealthy guilt and conflict and impedes healthy behavior. Let us look more closely at healthy and unhealthy ways of dealing with anger.

Psychological Anger

Unhealthy anger can be due to frustration with less than healthy needs or goals. Such unjust and unrealistic anger neither improves the situation nor promotes growth. For example, narcissistic persons are apt to become angry when they are not given what they want. They often assume that their needs supersede the needs of others, or that they are more important than others. When they drive, the road belongs to them and anyone who gets in the way evokes anger. Dependent people tend to manipulate people (usually unconsciously) for their satisfaction, and they become angry when people eventually withdraw from them. They will do anything to get others to nurture them and when people avoid their "sucking," they get angry. When narcissistic or dependent persons do not get their way, they become angry. Like any feeling, their anger tells them something about themselves: they are over- (narcissistic) or under- (dependent) estimating their worth.

A common form of unhealthy anger occurs when one's vulnerable identity is threatened. This frequently happens with inadequate persons who put on and hide behind an angry facade. When their defenses are weakened, especially by alcohol and/or a threatening person, they become irrationally angry, abusive, or violent. They try desperately to avoid and to compensate for their tenuous self-worth and control. Shame is often a buried motive for extreme anger.

A particular danger of unhealthy anger is to identify people with their negative traits or acts so that we see them only in terms of what we dislike. This totalizing process blocks out other qualities and possibilities and consequently limits or stops further discussion and growth. For example, a man who is hurt and angry over his neighbor's hostility may identify her with hostility, but seeing this neighbor only as a hostile person blinds him to her nonhostile acts. Actually, he is also hostile and his own hostility increases the likelihood of his neighbor's being hostile. Thus, he reinforces an endless repetition of hostility.

Anger may escalate into violence. Violent persons try to destroy others physically, psychologically, or spiritually. They may become so angry that they abuse and harm via insult, mockery, confusion, hate, indifference, or physical violence. Violent persons usually feel frustration, resentment, hurt, or inferiority, and their violence gives them feelings of unhealthy satisfaction, dignity, vindication, or superiority. Such unresolved feelings have probably accumulated over many years or decades and are periodically displaced on relatively innocent people.

Chronically angry people not only harm others, but they are especially destructive to themselves. Persistent anger violates the body, mind, emotions, and soul of oneself and others. Particularly in the forms of resentment and vindictiveness, anger is cancerous; it dissipates one's being. Furthermore, such angry people alienate other people, leaving them alone, lonely, and probably more frustrated and angry.

A common cause of unhealthy anger is to need someone to change in order to feel better. When our expectations are not met, we get angry, and we are often motivated to try to change the other. When we fail because we cannot change anyone (except ourselves), we are likely to get even angrier—actively or passively. Actively, we may become aggressive and attack the other person, or passively we may try to please or guilt the other person into submission. Even when the other person gives up, there is no victory, only seething hurt and anger. Needing others to change and, therefore, trying to control them results in alienation rather than community, in painful conflict rather than mutual serenity.

Unhealthy anger harms both ourselves and others and yet, with a healthy approach, it can be transformed into health. For instance, when we can be aware of our need for others to change, we can begin to work on accepting them as they are. Indeed, we can still want or prefer them to be different, but when we need them to be different, we are likely to be frustrated, feel unjustly treated, and get angry.

It is far better to get what we need from reliable others, from God, and from ourselves. For example, if we need respect from someone who is unwilling or unable to give it, we will be in trouble and we will likely get angry. It is as if we demand bread at a hardware store. Instead, we can respect ourselves and seek respect from God and reliable others. Such internal respect will enable us to accept and cope effectively with the hurtful person. Needing nothing from the person results in hurting less and managing better. Rather than anger, we reside in serenity.

Healthy anger is a realistic response to an unjust situation. A healthy form of anger could occur when people pull rank on us, especially rank they really do not have. Our anger can be a way of standing up for our dignity. Anger says, "I am not worthy of this treatment and I demand respect as a human being." Thus, anger sets boundaries to protect us and it affirms our basic worth. Such anger may also help unjust persons by telling them that they are not acting the way they should. Thus, one person's healthy anger may be an opportunity for another to improve. Rather than being chronic, controlling, and vindictive, healthy anger is temporary and in service of freedom and peace.

As with unhealthy anger, we must take a healthy approach toward healthy anger. It is common to take an unhealthy stand against our healthy anger. We can automatically get mad at ourselves for being mad. We can incorrectly assume that all anger is bad. We can be afraid of all anger because we have learned that anger evokes demeaning anger from others. We may have learned that anger always causes destruction. For whatever reason, we are unable to accept, listen to, and act constructively toward our (healthy) anger.

Anger can be a friend. When we slow down and respectfully and lovingly listen to our angry selves, we can learn to respond to our needs and hurts. To achieve this goal, we must look inside ourselves, not outside. Instead of getting the other people (outside) to be fair, respectful, loving, we respond to these needs within ourselves. Our consequent inner strength frees us from needing another person to change (to be fair, respectful, loving) and frees us to accept and live with unfair people. Anger becomes a good friend who faithfully reminds us to set boundaries that protect us and allows us to achieve the interior life of freedom and serenity.

Spiritual Anger

We can become really angry when we feel empty, bored, and frustrated, especially when we have diligently tried to live a good life. Suddenly, it seems, what recently made sense—namely, our lives—loses sense or is brought radically into question. After decades of trying to live the good life and feeling that we have taken the better path, we may wonder if we took the wrong one. Perhaps we feel that life has deceived us or we feel foolish and duped by life. We may be angry at God because we feel that God has deceived us or let us down.

Listen to this religious sister:

> I'm angry. And I hate to say it, but I'm angry at God. Here I am at fifty-two years old, in the religious life thirty-five years. I think I've been a pretty good nun. Not only have I been a fine teacher and principal, but I've also really tried to grow spiritually, to truly live the vowed and communal life. If I've done good, why don't I feel good?
>
> I feel like I'm in the middle of nowhere by myself. God? Where is He? I feel abandoned. Or maybe my whole life has been a hoax; maybe there is no God to abandon me. Yet I know there is. But where is He? I'm angry when I realize I have to work harder than ever. I'm angry when I feel stuck. I'm angry when parents don't support the faculty and criticize me. I'm angry when I'm too busy to take a vacation. Besides, I have no money. Most of all, I'm just angry. Why is life worse than ever? I thought it would be better. And I feel so alone. Nothing makes sense anymore. Where are you God? Why do you let me down?

We can become sick and tired of nothing, and we try to do something about it. Instead of escaping from the desert, it is better to listen to our anger, to learn what we are angry about, and to think about what can be done to protect and proclaim ourselves. For example, it would be helpful for the religious sister to accept and listen to her angry self. She can question some of her assumptions about life, such as the idea that a good life will bring justice. She can ask God to help her face the dark side of life and of herself as well as to mobilize her angry energy to protect and nurture her life. She can speak to God out of her anger. She might respectfully demand that God come to her rescue. Fighting with God might be a holy act. It is intimate. She may come to realize that her anger can lead her to a deeper relationship with God. Perhaps her anger is a gift from God that will help her renew her life.

Another possibility is that desert people can become hypercritical and even cynical when they observe people manipulating others for their own gains. Desert anger can give us an acute and passionate vision of life that may initially be one-sided. Our angry vision broadens to include not only the dark side of others but also our own shadow. By admitting the injustice and violence in ourselves and others, we are challenged to take opposite stands. We can work for justice and, even more important, become more loving and forgiving to others and especially to ourselves. Our anger can lead to a creative revolution to renew ourselves and others.

BOREDOM

In boredom, we find ourselves on pins and needles. We feel like jumping out of our skins. We cannot stand still in a meaningful way, and our actions neither make much sense nor get us anywhere. We use a lot of time and energy to do nothing and to go nowhere. We are tired of being on the psychological merry-go-round: going around in circles and getting nowhere. We are tired of being immobilized: trying to act but not being able to. We find ourselves in a bind: struggling to act in a meaningful way, but not experiencing any activity as appealing and meaningful. Consequently, we lack enthusiasm and lightness, and we feel edgy, heavy, and listless.

We feel trapped, condemned, or obligated to do something that is rather meaningless to us. Although we may look for some diversion, we still feel that we must do the thing we are bored with. A bored student feels obligated to study meaningless matters; a bored worker is compelled to do a job that makes no sense; a bored homemaker must clean and cook with little significance. Although they may procrastinate or withdraw from their tasks, they are obligated to return to their boring situations. Furthermore, their diversions often increase their tense emptiness, and they can easily feel frustrated about and angry at being locked in a senseless situation. A conflict emerges: bored people feel compelled to be where they are, but they want to be somewhere else.

Psychological Boredom

Unhealthy boredom can be seen with many neurotic people because they are compelled to repeat certain forms of unfruitful behavior. They tend to be phobic, obsessive-compulsive, hysterical, and overly dependent. In whatever case, neurotic people become bored with the same repetitious behavior that impedes a healthier and effective life. Neurotic persons typically ask the same questions and, consequently, get the same answers. They keep doing the same thing and expect different results.

Boredom can also be healthy. For instance, boredom with work may motivate us to change our jobs or our way or reason for working. Boredom urges us to find more meaning and comfort in or out of the job. Being bored with phony social situations could mean that we want no part of them. Instead of wasting time playing games, boredom motivates us to find something more productive and healthy.

Healthy boredom can motivate us to make life more meaningful. It pressures us to look at ourselves and at situations to discern what is really going on. For example, being bored at a business meeting may mean that we are irresponsible for not participating, the meeting may be repetitiously irrelevant, or the meeting is simply out of our range of interests. Students may be bored with a class because they have no interest in the class, they are not prepared, the teacher has a wooden, mesmerizing style, or the subject is not interesting to them. Whatever the case, boredom is a source of truth that can help us to manage better and thus improve our lives.

Spiritual Boredom

In the throes of nothingness, we feel locked in a meaningless existence. We feel trapped in a dark room with no exit. Paradoxically, and patiently, we discover in time that light emerges from the darkness and that an exit is no longer necessary. Then spiritual boredom (nothing making sense) eventually leads to genuine enthusiasm (living in sense).

Spiritual boredom means that nothing appeals to us. We are bored with superficiality, manipulation, and convention; they have no appeal for us. Nothingness motivates to us to bore through and transcend these realities to experience more lasting and significant experiences. In spiritual boredom, we try to bore deeper into life by constantly questioning and searching for deeper meaning. Our boredom is a creative repetition, not a compulsive repetition.

Boredom pressures us to question and reflect on our assumptions about the spiritual life as well as to deepen, expand, and modify ourselves. Boredom can be a wake-up call to transform our spiritual selves, to make our spiritual lives more vital and relevant. Instead of purging or numbing boredom, we accept the gift of boredom and allow it to lead us to a better way.

We can be bored with religious rituals and excesses that once made sense. Practices that made helpful sense for decades now become boring. What once worked leaves us empty. Rather than giving up such practices, our boredom can be a challenge to discover new ways that nurture us. Our boredom asks us to renew ourselves so that what was once very good can get better. We are called to bore deeper into reality.

Spiritual boredom can lead to a deeper relationship with God. Sometimes spiritual ideas and practices that once made sense no longer make much sense. Our way to God gets stale. And yet, we may know no other way. Feeling stuck in such a situation is uncomfortable, but our boredom challenges us to renew our relationship with God. With faith and patience, we can bore through the desert to a better land.

Spiritual boredom presents God in absence. Rather than purging our boredom, we allow ourselves to be bored. We accept boredom as a paradoxical gift from God, as an opportunity to become more intimate with God. Boredom calls for faith and patience to accept and wait for our renewal in God. Spiritual boredom eventually leads to enthusiasm (*en theo* means "in God" in Greek).

APATHY

The etymology of apathy denotes a lack of suffering, passion, and concern. Apathy, however, is not lifelessness, but is a peculiar and paradoxical feeling that connotes the pain of not suffering, the passion of being passionless, and the difference in being indifferent.

Apathy is the feeling of not feeling anything, or of feeling nothing. We do not feel one way or another. We are not interested. We are neither turned on nor turned off. A thirty-two-year-old woman expressed herself this way: "I don't feel anything. I just don't feel positive or negative. It's like I don't care anymore. I feel kind of detached—in it, but not of it. Although I feel kind of empty, I feel okay and, in a sense, free. Yes, I guess that is a feeling. Like, it's feeling nothing."

Apathy may emerge out of a long struggle, out of satisfaction, or out of indifference. After much pain, we may let go of our suffering and become apathetic. Instead of tearing ourselves apart, we feel calmly indifferent. We may try to deny our anguish by not feeling at all. We may also be apathetic because we are satisfied. Satiated people, for instance, are apathetic toward more food; sexually satisfied persons do not care for more sex; contented persons may not search for more meaning. Such apathetic people have had enough; any more is senseless.

We may not have an interest in an activity because we never had the opportunity to learn to be interested. Some people are apathetic toward classical music and others are indifferent to rock 'n roll because of a lack of exposure. Their lack of interest is neither healthy nor unhealthy; it is simply not an issue for them. Also, the culture reinforces gender apathy toward certain behavior. For example, men are often apathetic toward chitchat or rapport dialogue, while most women show less interest in task-oriented or report conversation.

Psychological Apathy

Unhealthy apathy may be a symptom of pathological processes. People who rigidly repress feelings are not affectively interested or interesting. They lack vitality and passion, and their presence is insipid and flat. For example, schizoid persons who withdraw from competitive and intimate relationships are coldly distant and hide behind masks of apathy.

Some people become apathetic toward significant and lasting values, and learn to adjust to a shallow life. They miss many opportunities, particularly in the areas of intimacy with themselves and others, and with life in general. Such apathy says to a person, "Listen! You are running from crucial experiences. Instead of moving into life, you are becoming lifeless. Why do you lack enthusiasm in your life? Is it really necessary to live lifelessly?"

A healthy form of psychological apathy often occurs when an experience does not fit into our lifestyles. For example, pornography simply may not excite us because we see it as not healthy or because it does not make much sense to us. We feel bland, indifferent, and empty toward it. Such healthy apathy engenders freedom from impediments and a freedom for healthy experiences.

Spiritual Apathy

Spiritual apathy often occurs when nothing makes sense. The desert depths may numb our bodies and level our rationality. Sometimes we may feel alive but dead, like zombies. All our dogmas, beliefs, theories, and ideas may lose sense. They no longer give us answers, fulfill us, or make any real difference. All the things that once gave pleasure, contentment, achievement, and success become inadequate responses to nothingness. "No-thing" excites us.

In desert nothingness, we may get bored with being bored, tired of being frustrated, and become apathetic. We get sick and tired of suffering. Again, the paradox is that our apathy is a purifying process that empties us for greater fulfillment. Our *a-pathos* (lack of passion) is in service of *pathos* (passion).

A forty-three-year-old man expressed himself this way:

> I don't care anymore. I'm tired of making sense of everything, sick of trying to change things. I've had enough of people pulling rank on me, not accepting me. I'm tired of running and escaping with work, booze, and sex. I've stopped. Yes, I feel kind of lost, empty, and scared. But I'm no longer knocking my head against a wall; so, I don't have a headache. Not feeling much feels pretty good. Somehow I feel lighter and

> stronger. I'm involved, but also kind of detached. It's like a detached attachment. Yet I feel more in touch. It's like I see more clearly.

Some desert people become apathetic toward old structures and ways of behaving. Instead of becoming frustrated, bored, or angry with certain forms of institutional religion, they become apathetic. In a sense, they take a spiritual leave of absence. Whether their apathy occurs after a long struggle or emerges more suddenly, their challenge is to remain open to and listen to their apathy, and pursue other avenues of meaning.

Listen to this young mother:

> The church, the liturgy, the people—they used to make me angry. Now, I don't care. I can't even get turned off. I'm turned off already. Although I'm concerned about being unconcerned, I think I can be religious in other ways. Yet, I'm concerned about my baby. Should I fake enthusiasm for his sake? Is the home enough? Maybe by the time he is older, I'll find some sense in religion. Anyhow, I have to be honest with myself. But I also want to be fair to him.

In spiritual apathy, everything is equal—a zero. Nothing makes sense. We feel emptied, cut off, silenced, and ignorant. The slate is clean. Although we are not passionately involved, our affective indifference is positive. We are apathetic toward everything because nothing can give us what we long for. Our apathy is a gateway to enthusiasm.

A power greater than ourselves is hidden in our powerlessness. Accepting our apathy enables us to connect with the source of pathos—the passionate God of our understanding. God not only comes to us but is already with us in our apathetic nothingness. In the arid and empty desert, there is nothing to impede God's presence. In time and with God, the listless spirit is refreshed, consoled, and renewed.

ANGUISH

Perhaps our deepest suffering is anguish. In anguish, we intensely feel pain that seems to make little or no sense. We feel immersed in and shackled by pain. We feel so depressed that we can only scream; so lonely that we feel hopelessly cut off; so anxious that we are torn apart. In anguish, we ask, "Why?" and get the response of absurdity. We ask, "How?" and feel helpless. We ask, "When will it end?" and are given uncertainties. We ask, "Where is there peace?" and we are left lost. We feel overwhelmed and on the verge of helplessness. We feel trapped with no exit. We feel beat up and beaten. We wonder if we can take any more. We feel encompassed by and permeated with fear and anxiety. We have hit bottom. We have descended to hell.

Psychological Anguish

Unhealthy anguish is a price we eventually pay for saying, "no" to significant aspects of life. Our "no" to life is self-destructive. For example, neurotic persons may fight themselves so much that they feel uselessly tired and meaninglessly sick. Their compulsion to repeat the same fruitless patterns of behavior become a living hell. Some people are so pressured by the burdens of guilt and shame that they feel like giving up or falling apart. Their heavy, negative, and irritating lives progressively strangle them.

The anguish of losing control, of being helpless, and of not being able to function threatens to implode us. We may tremble in fear of losing contact, of breaking down, and staying down. We are petrified of being shattered to pieces that cannot be reassembled. The fear of becoming psychotic is filled with anguish.

People lacking authentic values, significant activities, and healthy love live in the shadow of anguish. Although they may be able to cope, their lives become precarious, empty, and meaningless as they grow older. Their lack of a valid reason for living evokes a suffocating anguish and their lives can turn into a desperate attempt to escape from the throes of anguish. Addictions, especially, are futile attempts to escape anguish.

Healthy anguish is a response to overwhelming absurdity. Sometimes, an experience seems to make no sense, is unjust, does not fit, or is too powerful. Sometimes, the most appropriate response is to suffer with dignity because life is absurd. What do parents do when their only child is born severely retarded and physically deformed? Hopefully, they can accept and transcend their anguish by caring for and loving the child. Although their anguish may not totally disappear, it does become manageable and may even foster inner- and interpersonal strength.

A healthy form of anguish can clearly be seen in the sudden death of a loved one. Parents feel anguished over the death of their child. They feel the sudden rush of the incomprehensible and uncontrollable. The situation is out of their hands; nothing can be done. They are depressed and torn apart. "Why?" evokes no answer. Anguish can be the most appropriate response.

Spiritual Anguish

In the throes of desert nothingness, we may feel spiritual anguish. Being painfully alone, anxiously nowhere, and depressingly lost throws us into anguish. We feel the pain of living. And yet, anguish can lead to joy. We will see that the anguish of coming-to-death can evoke and promote a richer appreciation of life. To minister to our groaning spirit can lead to more serenity.

Although we may feel overwhelmed with pain, our suffering can be a breakdown that is in service of a breakthrough. To live in anguish is to live in a broken world. Everything is smashed into nonsense. Although the storm of anguish wrecks everything, the storm can clear, and renewal and rebuilding can begin. When we accept and listen to our sobs, we begin to let go and let God comfort our groaning spirit, and the storm settles and new growth occurs. Similar to apathy (the polar opposite of anguish), anguish levels everything and empties us for the gift of serenity.

We may feel alone in our anguish. Everyone, including God, seems to have abandoned us in this hell on earth. We cry out to the God of comfort and consolation. Sometimes God responds overtly and sometimes God feels absent. During these times of desolation, we must reach out to God's people while waiting for God's healing. Remember that God's people do not try to change or "fix" others to make them "healthy" or feel better. God's people follow God's Word, accept it, and compassionately journey with anguished souls. In patience, we can know that God is always with us if not overtly, then covertly. God is with us in our anguish and eventually will lead us through this painful land to more serene places.

Only God can save us. God alone, or in others, can comfort and console us. Our breakdown of the illusion of self-sufficiency and self-control leads to a breakthrough to more power, control, and care. This darkest night leads to light and warmth. Descending to the bottom is the way to ascend to the top.

Chapter 5

Adolescence

Moving from childhood to adolescence involves many changes. If childhood was safe, secure, and satisfying, we may make this transition rather smoothly. If childhood was unhealthy or turbulent, adolescence is likely to be fraught with problems. Also, the health of childhood is no guarantee of the kind of adolescence that we may have. Still, for better or for worse, childhood is significant to adolescence and adulthood.

Adolescence presents a myriad of changes—physical, psychosocial, and spiritual. Developmental changes are clearly manifested in our bodies, our feelings, thinking, interpersonal relationships, spirituality, and identities. Our bodies, including sexuality, change dramatically. Thinking expands into more abstract, formal operations. Feelings, moods, and emotions are experienced more deeply, intensely, and extensively. Spirituality becomes more explicit and significant. People look at and relate to us differently; we are no longer seen or treated as children. We look and act differently. We are coming of age.

DESERT OF DISENCHANTMENT

Physical and psychosocial changes from childhood to adolescence engender new experiences. Old and new feelings are often intense as well as ambivalent and ambiguous. Particularly as young adolescents, we can be aimless and restless, lacking goals and ideals. Although we have boundless and impetuous energy, we also become frustrated and tired. We may shrug our shoulders in apathy.

The initial desert of nothingness occurs in adolescence, and it is often seen most clearly in the sophomore year of high school—the year of the "wise fool." Although we have lived no more than a decade and a half, we seem to be bored with life, for nothing seems to appeal to us. We keep looking for new things to do and almost anything exciting seems to turn us on; nevertheless, we quickly end up in the same position—bored.

In early adolescence, it is not rare to become cynical, or at least critical of parents and other authorities. We are prone to proclaim with Holden Caulfield as he says in *The Catcher in the Rye:* "The whole damn world is phony." We may take special delight in trying to make authorities feel uncomfortable. We too, however, feel discontent because we suspect and criticize the very people we must depend on. We are burdened and challenged by a classic bind of trying to break away from the people on whom we still depend.

Structure is a special reminder of our *lack* of structure, and we want no part of it. In fact, some of us think of ways of breaking rules and irritating authorities. Structured people, who seem to know where they are going, make us anxious and angry. Such adults seem to know everything, instead of nothing. In our critical and oppositional styles, we discover how we can challenge others' thinking and influence their feelings. In short, new ways of perceiving, thinking, judging, feeling, relating, and behaving are emerging.

Although as young adolescents we spend considerable time with our peers, we feel that no one really understands us. Being in this precarious place, we begin to realize that it is ultimately up to us to make sense of life. When nobody and nothing make much sense, our world feels like a cosmos of nonsense. It is up to us to make order and sense of our lives. Unlike childhood, nobody except ourselves can do it for us. A new responsibility is emerging.

Understandably, in this phase of adolescence, we seem to be edgy, irritable, and mopey. The security of our recent past has vanished; our future feels nonexistent; and our present time is in the flux of nothingness. While our old ways are gone and new ways are not yet developed, we find ourselves in the anxious situation of being nowhere. Everything, including ourselves is in suspension; we have nothing to hold, and nothing is clear. We are desert novices.

Religion may become a special target for oppositional criticism. Some adolescents get mad at religious people who demand that adolescents follow adult abstractions that have little relevance to them. For others, religion simply turns them off, for there is little appeal or motivation to turn them on. In comparison to mass-media entertainment, religious services feel boring.

Some adolescents, however, challenge religious leaders to make religion more meaningful. Most religions try to respond to this challenge with a ministry that speaks to adolescents. The degrees of success of such programs partially depend on understanding the worlds of adolescents. And since early, middle, and late adolescents are worlds apart, religious ministry to adolescents is indeed difficult, challenging, and important.

Ideally, religion is in service of the adolescent's spiritual life. To appreciate that young adolescents are likely to be bored with or critical of the spiritual is important. Giving them the opportunity to hear a different voice than the media, as well as a voice that they can understand, may not make much overt difference at the present moment, but may plant seeds for future growth. Remember that young adolescents are letting go of their childhood answers and have not yet formulated their own. Thus, it is critical to journey in their nothingness to help them traverse this initial desert with people who practice the spiritual life. Since the attitudes and values we form in adolescence usually carry us through life, exposure to spirituality is significant to later development.

The desert of adolescent nothingness is usually confusing to almost everyone. Parents are often taken aback by the sudden change in their child and, too often, they interpret, with good intentions, the experience as negative. In one way, the desert is a negative experience because it is filled with emptiness and loss. But as we have proposed, nothingness is decidedly positive and essential for growth. It behooves parents to accept and understand their children's stressful metamorphosis as well as hold them responsible for appropriate behavior.

If parents have escaped or denied their own desert experiences, their adolescent children are likely to threaten or unsettle them by evoking their own submerged and unresolved experiences. In this kind of situation, more parental harm than help is likely to occur. Such parents may sincerely give their children negative injunctions to escape or reject their desert experiences. A common approach is to judge their experience as something to be gotten rid of. Although their transition can be problematic, disruptive, and stressful, it is a mainly positive experience to be accepted.

Teachers who deal with pupils in nothingness, such as sophomores, are challenged to work productively and creatively. It is important to be willing and able to enter their adolescent desert to help them accept and make sense of their experience. On the other hand, teachers who demand rigid order and clarity at all times are likely to evoke opposition and resentment. Effective teachers (and parents) are able to challenge students and hold them accountable while moving with the apparent nonsense of nothingness.

How we deal with nothingness in adolescence is crucial for later development. The attitudes and approaches we solidify in adolescence tend to carry us throughout life. Fortunately, youth and naive openness make it less likely for adolescents to reject, distort, and deny their experiences than in later stages of development. The adolescent's resiliency and ignorance decrease the possibilities of pathological coping mechanisms.

Too many adolescents, however, cope ineffectively. For example, some children control or hide serious problems behind a veneer of quiet obedience but, when they experience the stress and demands of adolescence, they manifest problems. Some children never reach the desert of adolescence because they regress to an earlier level of development. Others may try to circumvent their desert selves by acting as if they are older. Some are too needy or wounded to experience the desert.

Although adolescents usually emerge out of nothingness in a year or two, some get fixated in it. An example is a person in his fourth decade who is still aimlessly roaming the earth in an adolescent nothingness. Such a thirty-five-year-old is still sophomoric in his criticism of structures and authorities that are threatening and alien to his diffused life.

Addiction and violence are common ways to escape and numb desert pain. Most addictive adolescents are quite intelligent, gifted, and sensitive; their awareness, confusion, and pain may be more than normal. Whatever the situation, alcohol, other drugs, and sex are available means of relieving pain and gaining temporary fulfillment. Since the apparent "gains" are very short term, such coping only serves to engender more confusion, self-alienation, and shame as well as the dire consequences of addiction.

Violence is another human, but inadequate, response. Some adolescents take on a negative identity, feeling that being good at being bad is better than being nobody. Such violent coping and negative identity formation particularly solidify and escalate with group support and activity. Achieving a healthy identity is made more difficult, frustrating, and frightening when there is little helpful structure and support from parents and other authorities. Such a situation increases the likelihood of psychological and social problems.

Most adolescents manage to stay out of serious trouble and come to a sense of identity that enables them to cope effectively and achieve success. From a functional perspective, most young adolescents do moderately well with the present and for the future. The spiritual perspective, however, is often minimized or forgotten. Cultural and media forces, such as individualism and moral relativism, militate against the spiritual being paramount in one's life. In spite of such deterrents, the desert of adolescent nothingness usually leads to a land of new possibilities.

LAND OF ENCHANTMENT

In a relatively short time, our nothingness leads us to a new way of being. Before this time, even though we may have been mature for our age, we were basically "preauthentic" with respect to spiritual experiences such as love, compassion, and commitment. Our adumbrated presence to spirituality in childhood is foundational and significant, but its covert presence is not the same as in adulthood. In childhood, spirituality comes primarily from outside ourselves, whereas, in adolescence and adulthood, spirituality comes primarily from within ourselves.

Clearly, our childhood exposure to spirituality influences our later, overt experiences of spirituality. Role models, particularly parents, are perhaps the most critical factors in a child's formation. This kind of religious education can also facilitate or impede later spiritual development. For example, either an authoritarian or a laissez-faire approach in childhood would probably have detrimental effects on adolescent and adult spirituality.

The acute experience of adolescent nothingness seems to disappear as quickly as it appears. Our bored and empty existence has prepared us for a life that can be enthusiastic and meaningful. In middle or late adolescence, we come out of the desert and begin to experience spirituality more explicitly and overtly. We come out of the shadows to a more enlightened way of experiencing reality. Indeed, we are novices of spirituality, but we have begun to travel a new road.

Our new presence to spirituality manifests itself in various ways. For example, personal subjects such as literature and religion take on new and deeper meaning. Personal journal writing or, at least, reflective thought are not uncommon. An adolescent's intense concern and respect for individual rights implies an understanding of individual conscience. In whatever case, we begin to experience and think more deeply about life.

Spirituality affects the moral realm. For instance, we experience a new guilt, not because we break a rule or because we feel we will be punished, but because we violate a person. Rather than aiming to clean our slate of conscience, our guilt motivates us toward reconciliation and creative restitution. Rather than perfunctory penance or apology, we try, in some way, to make appropriate amends.

Instead of being bored, we often retire meaningfully into solitude. We may see solitude as a way of listening to and reflecting on spiritual experiences, and we may begin a journal in which we meditate on and write about our discoveries. Although we have heard about the poetic, we now begin to experience it. Spiritual meaning not only speaks from without, but it now begins to resonate from within us.

For example, autonomy and freedom develop more fully. Rather than merely following external laws, *our* law begins to come more from within ourselves. This beginning of autonomy (*autos,* "self"; *nomos,* "law") leads to a new freedom. Although we may have felt free, our freedom was mainly a "freedom from" rather than a "freedom for." We are now becoming the true authors of our lives—authentic persons. The call to be committed also speaks to us for the first time. We realize that a challenging life lies ahead of us, and to live it well takes commitment.

Life opens up transrationally. We see that the deeper dimensions of living have little to do with rationality and logic. The paradoxical begins to play with us; the possible fascinates us; and the mysterious entices us. Although we cannot explain these experiences, we can accept, listen, and follow them. Along with a deeper appreciation of nature, the fine and performing arts may evoke an aesthetic sense of wonder that opens up our spirituality. Indeed, these experiences may *not* occur but, when they do, they are just beginning to develop.

In this novitiate of spirituality, we begin to generate compassion, an understanding responsibility, and respect. We begin to sense that love is not just fun or satisfying, but that it includes suffering and sacrifice. We get an inkling of kinship with others so that violence, injustice, and crime evoke different thinking and feeling.

Sometimes this relatively exciting and intense presence to life elicits a romantic idealism. Since we are enthusiastic about what life can and ought to be, we may lose sight of life's limits and become enchanted with everything. Instead of nothing making sense, everything makes sense. Particularly if we are prone to perfectionism, we may have difficulty accepting imperfections. We might even become scrupulous, or rigid and literal, in our ideals. In time, our ideal and romantic vision is tempered with reality.

Responsibility is another issue. We realize that our ability to respond to responsibility is primarily in our hands. Rules and structures now take on new meanings. We begin to internalize their meanings. Unfair structures and social impediments of the past are now seen as challenges to change. Instead of feeling like a victim of the system or simply complaining about it, we begin to think of ways to improve things or to make a difference. Unlike children, we are becoming aware that our well-being is primarily our responsibility, and we can do something about it.

Religion and morality are often important issues. Youths desire deeper meaning in their ethical and religious life. It is common for seniors in high school to pursue new ways or challenge old ways of religious meaning. They want more concrete ways of experiencing God, or they become critical about their religion, and many drift away from formal religion. With or without religion, spirituality takes on new meaning.

God often comes out of the shadows and into the light. The meaning of life, how to and why to live, afterlife, and religion come into question and are usually in reference to God. "How can God make a difference in my life?" is a key question. We want an experiential God who is relevant to our lives. Abstract gods make little sense. If not enchanted with God, we demand at least a God who speaks our language; otherwise, there are many substitutes to take God's place.

The important point is that, as we grow in adolescence, we seek to deepen religious meaning. We can no longer conform as children, but we now want to experience a God who makes a relevant impact on our lives. We demand an experiential God who makes a difference; a theoretical God is not good enough. Indeed, like the rest of our lives, God may be romanticized. We want to feel and engage an ideal God who helps us to feel, think, and live better. Or we want no God at all.

One of the paramount tasks of adolescence is to form an identity that incorporates new vision, thinking, and feeling. Some adolescents form a negative identity, feeling that negativity is better than being no one. Still others are stuck in a moratorium, searching to find themselves. Meanwhile, a few take on another identity (foreclosure) and thereby stop their own self-searching.

Whatever path we take, the presence or absence of spirituality makes a significant difference. Those who incorporate healthy values in their identities are more able to commit personally and professionally later in life, and are more likely to abstain from unhealthy and illegal behavior. If we begin to develop a spiritual life, we are likely to manage better and to be happier than without one.

When spirituality is part of identity, genuine ethical living becomes very important. To act simply to get a reward or to escape punishment is unlikely. Although we have few answers, we have many ethical questions: How can I make a good impact on the world? What is right and wrong for me? What makes an action good or bad? Is everything morally relative? Are there objective standards? What is the relationship between the letter and the spirit of the law? Although such questions may be difficult to articulate, they are felt.

In a certain sense, our adolescent insights remain primarily within ourselves because, personally and environmentally, we are not yet ready to implement our ideas. We are preparing to express ourselves and to make our way in life. It is important, however, that we think and talk about our insights before we try to implement them. Thus, although cognitively and spiritually we can see life's limits and possibilities better than before, we are probably not ready to make important decisions about ourselves or others.

Our theme has been that we initially encounter our deeper selves in and through the desert of adolescent nothingness. Nothingness evokes a radical change in the direction and style of our being. Before this time, our spiritual experiences were preauthentic in that they set the foundation for later, authentic experiences. Although we are neophytes, we are beginning to be called within ourselves to live spiritually and to take the responsibility to be virtuous. This time in our spiritual odyssey is usually short, for soon another desert and promised land await us.

Chapter 6

Young Adulthood

So, you're graduating from high school. That's great. What are you going to do? Where are you going to live? Are you going to college? Which one? Do you have a major? Who's going to pay for it? Do you have a summer job? What do your parents think? You're lucky. Good luck!

Oh, you're not going to college. Why not? What are you going to do? How are you going to live? Are you moving away from home? Do you have a job? Is it a good one? What about a career? Don't join the service. Don't get married. Make money. Travel. Get established. Live it up. Take your time. But don't waste time. Be careful; it's a hard life. But you're young. You're really lucky. The best of luck!

Such monologues dramatize the pressure of the many expectations typical of the transition from the adolescence to young adulthood. A bit before or soon after high school graduation, older adolescents enter a new era. They experience significant environmental and social changes involving new role expectations. These young people feel the uncomfortable, yet exciting, transition between not quite being young adults and no longer being adolescents. Older adolescents stand on the brink of young adulthood.

Most young adults who enter the worlds of work and/or higher education must adjust to people of various socioeconomic backgrounds, ethnic groups, and races as well as new work, educational, recreational, and living opportunities. Some young adults experience difficulties; most, however, manage to make the necessary adjustments. As these adjustments are made, another desert looms on the horizon.

DESERT OF DISCOVERY

Most of us, sometime in our late teens or early twenties, experience what can be called a crisis of young adulthood. As in all passages, not everyone undergoes a crisis, but many do—some severely and some mildly. It can be a time when we, to some degree, confront ourselves and radically reevaluate the meaning of our lives. We ask crucial questions of ourselves: Who am I? Where am I going? Whence do I come? What's life all about? However, not infrequently, these questions go unheard or unheeded because of our noisy busyness. Too seldom do we take time to listen and respond to them. Let us listen.

It is a time when adolescent values are questioned and modified, and when everything and everyone, including ourselves, are thrown into question. Once again, desert themes emerge. Nothing much makes sense. No particular thing may feel as fulfilling or meaningful as it was in the later years of adolescence. Instead of acquiring answers, the focus now is on asking questions and questioning answers. Sense that recently gave us direction and possibilities now recedes into the background. What we thought we had suddenly seems to slip away. We are called to find new ways to form ourselves and our lives. What is important? To what end does one choose and act? What difference will my decisions make? Indeed, if our values and commitments—our lives—go unexamined, we are likely to live relatively shallow and meaningless lives. Such issues are, at least in part, spiritual.

In becoming adults, we are on our way to finding our pace and place in life. Paradoxically, out of feeling that we are "no one" and living "nowhere," we actually discover more of who we are and where we are called to be. It is not easy, however, to journey through this desert, particularly if we are used to getting what we want when we want it. The desert experience challenges a life of self-centeredness and indulgence.

This desert journey is often lonely. On empty and quiet nights, we hear, deep within ourselves, questions: Can I give to and receive from another person? Will I ever be genuinely intimate with another person? With whom? Where? How? When? We reach out, but our touch falls short. We speak, but no one hears. We listen, but we hear nothing.

Because of past interpersonal experiences, we may be frightened to death of what we want most—intimacy. Or we may simply feel helpless or ignorant about how to know people. We may discover that we feel misunderstood and unknown, perhaps because we feel unworthy and ashamed to share ourselves. Whatever the reason, only we hear our silent screams for love. We yearn for the healing presence of another person. Though we may feel afraid, helpless, or unworthy, we want to reach out—to touch and to be touched.

Spiritual loneliness is essential to coming to love. It purifies us for the gift of one another and ultimately for God. In and through loneliness, we become aware of ourselves so we can share ourselves more fully and deeply. We begin to realize, often unconsciously, that God is at the center of our lives. In the quiet yearning of loneliness, we can hear whispers of a divine call. We hear a hint and feel a nudge to go beyond the ordinary.

Self-confrontation in loneliness is a crisis of loving and, ultimately, of being loved. In this advent of mature love, we ask ourselves: Can I love myself? Can I love another? Can I live the true spirit of life, that is, love? Am I worthy of love? Can I be loved no matter what? Does love exist for me? If God is really love, then does God exist? Will I always be lonely? Will my questions ever be answered? Without such questions and without such dark nights of loneliness, it is difficult and perhaps impossible to live an authentic life of love.

Without love, life becomes bland and listless, lacking in enthusiasm or spirit. The paradox is that, as young adults, we must travel the deserts of loneliness to enjoy the lands of love. The ever present dangers are to accept counterfeits of love or to numb the liberating pain of loneliness. Escapes from loneliness are available, numerous, and tempting. Sex, work, power, and drugs, for instance, can silence the summons of loneliness so that love is forgotten in service of stagnant comfort.

We have seen that a common danger is to judge our feelings as negative, resulting in feeling guilty about conditions that are psychologically and spiritually healthy. Rather than accepting our feelings, we repress or numb them. To combat such negative approaches is not easy. Delaying satisfaction, in service of facing ourselves, can seem senseless if we are used to having our needs satisfied. Some of us pursue pleasure and others repress experiences. "Letting it all hang out" or holding our feelings "in," we fail to listen to our nothingness. Neither the life of license nor the life of restriction are likely to lead to healthy serenity.

Spiritual as well as psychological stress challenges our mental health and both can activate latent problems. If, through childhood and adolescence, latent processes have been held in check, they are likely to emerge at this time. For instance, those who are basically compulsive may become more compulsive under the stress of spiritual change. Consider persons who come from overly protective homes. Uprooting and crisis can leave them so precariously on their own that they fail to cope. Uncharacteristic, extreme behavior, such as promiscuous sexuality, drug abuse, or isolation, is not uncommon.

Another danger is to act extremely "independent" as a reaction to parental and other authorities as well as an effort to solidify one's identity. As an attempt to free ourselves from dependence, we try to live completely on our own. Physical and social independence, however, does not guarantee psychological and spiritual independence. In fact, mature independence includes a certain kind of dependence wherein we freely choose to be interdependent.

In the desert, away from the marketplace, we realize that spiritual living involves exploring our true source of worth. We discover that to feel radically worthwhile, no matter what occurs, depends more on our spiritual roots than on our social status. Social pressures to succeed professionally and personally, to meet the demands of everyday living, and to look good can obscure and short-circuit learning opportunities in the desert.

Conventional morality is questioned and challenged even more deeply in young adulthood than in adolescence. Rather than conforming to rules and expectations of society just because they are conventional, we become acutely aware of individual rights and values. This period of questioning can be part of the process that leads to a "postconventional" approach toward morality. This approach goes beyond the external rewards and punishments of preconventional morality and the conformist, or "law and order," conventional morality. More people are apt to subscribe to the conventional, following the law rather than its spirit. Others seize upon a self-serving morality by doing what feels "good." Yet another approach is for people to regress to an earlier mode of morality when they are under pressure or faced with responsibility. For instance, young adults who become parents often regress to what they previously criticized as their parents' "old fashioned and authoritarian morals." According to Lawrence Kohlberg (1969), some adults reach the final stage of moral development known as the "universal ethical principle level."

Carol Gilligan (1984) originally a student of Kohlberg, gives a moral perspective that balances male-oriented theories such as Kohlberg's and Freud's with insights gained from interviews with females. In brief, Gilligan found that most females make moral decisions according to an ethic of care in contrast to a male ethic of justice. She discovered that women tend to speak of morality in terms of compassion and their responsibilities to themselves and others. The female sense of connectedness lends itself to care and compassion in contrast to the male separateness that engenders a framework of rights and justice.

According to Gilligan, adolescence involves a shift from care of self to care of others, which eventually can lead to a transition to caring for "us"—both self and others. There is a risk that females will lose or weaken their identities by minimizing their ethic of care and connectedness and absorbing the more male approach of separation and justice. Thus, adolescence and young adulthood can be more problematic for females than for males.

Both moral approaches are important. They ought to complement each other, not be mutually exclusive. The danger is to lose the female vision of morality and thus become fragmented rather than whole or androgynous. One without the other weakens male and female identity as well as society's.

From a spiritual perspective, authentic morality is not only a function of cognitive development, but also of spirituality. For instance, the formation of virtue, particularly love, significantly influences our moral lives. In some respects, the female ethic of care and compassion lends itself more to spirituality than the male cognitive ethic of rights and justice. Justice is the protector of spirituality, whereas compassion is its expression. Both approaches—care (the heart, spirituality, mysterious, interpersonal, process) and justice (the head, cognitive, problematic, task-oriented, content)—are needed. Justice can be seen as the minimum demand of care and care can be construed as the motivator of justice.

Conflict between morals and mores also erupts. For example, if a young man values celibacy and yet, under pressure, apologizes for being celibate, he is caught between contending values. It is difficult to live with integrity especially when our leaders, mass media, cultures, reference groups, or communities practice morals that differ from our own. It takes courage and conviction to live by one's standards regardless of the presence or absence of cultural and environmental support. Achieving a solid sense of self that is part of and nourished by a community is critical to following norms that differ from those of the mainstream. Conversely, a diffused identity increases the likelihood of following or being controlled by conventional norms or the mass mentality.

There are several popular ways to resolve moral conflict. One is the way of relativism. We say that everything is relative (depending on situational factors) and that nothing is objective or absolute. However, we fail to realize that this principle *is* an objective absolute. Another view offers the test of "honesty and sincerity," which posits that, as long as one is honest and sincere, the behavior is good. However, we *can* forget that sin can be honest and sincere. Some try to become amoral, often implying that reason can handle everything and that guilt is an unnecessary impediment. The moral imperative of this rationalism is to be without moral qualms. Such moral approaches are the norm in mass media. It is the exception to see moral decisions made on the basis of spiritual conviction.

Most desert travelers also question religion. Some of us become quite critical of religious institutions, their practices, and their members. Young adults are especially critical of phoniness, double standards, and ready-made solutions. Religious hypocrites—those who act religiously in church but are not spiritual with others—are especially irritating. In reaction, some young adults become agnostic and doubt everything, or they try out new religions. Still, many young adults want to be touched by religion, desiring it to be experiential rather than just theoretical. They want to be fulfilled with virtue rather than with ideas.

Along with religion, the desert brings God into question. Some young adults take a humanistic position rather than a spiritual one, stating that life can be meaningful without a transcendent God. Life's meaning is totally in one's hands. Others try to be indifferent to any spiritual quest by regarding God as a dead issue or an illusion. Consequently, God becomes more absent than present. Many simply forget God in their busy pursuit of success and become lax in their spiritual pursuits. The lack of spiritual living results in dire consequences, such as a shorter and emptier life.

In seeking a mature stand, young adults find themselves immersed in a multitude of views. Many were raised without clear values, or to think that all views are equal, or to assume that what feels comfortable is good or right. Instead of having a strong value system to criticize and explore, they are left with nothing much to examine. Dialogue becomes silent and growth is consequently stunted.

What it means to be a man or a woman is another key desert issue. What is the relationship of sex to gender and how to integrate them? "Who am I?" and "Who can I be?" are both spiritual as well as sexual questions. Some adults find religion to be helpful in responding to these sexual-spiritual issues. Probably more people divorce themselves from religion, feeling that religion is a hindrance or not helpful. Some mistakenly identify spiritually with religion and, thus, impede their personal and interpersonal growth.

Desert processes also evoke questions about genital sex. For instance, what approach does a young adult take toward genital feelings? Repress them? Satisfy them? Can they really be integrated? How? Few know how to relate sexuality to spirituality. Some young adults postpone such issues and often repress their genital feelings. Many young adults (and adolescents) satisfy them prematurely and unauthentically. Not many of any age bring sexuality into harmony with their psychosocial-spiritual selves.

Besides reaching their genital peak, many men tend to maximize genital sexuality, while minimizing the other more basic aspects of sexuality—feelings that lead to intimacy, but not necessarily to genital sex. Many young men have been taught to assume that physical affection is only in service of genital sexuality. Thus, they have problems in expressing affective sexuality as an end in itself without somehow leading to genital satisfaction. Such sexual programming is a serious obstacle to spiritual growth, for it often inhibits intimate sharing and love.

Although in the past, young women were taught to experience affective sexuality as an end in itself, contemporary women more freely use affection as an end, or as a means to genital sexuality. Thus, many women are freer than men in expressing affection, which is usually a positive, though often frustrating, factor in their spiritual lives.

Among the main obstacles to spiritual health are the "desert demons," which are negative injunctions from self and others. Frequently, we feel guilty for positive and necessary feelings. For instance, it is difficult to feel lonely without some sense of guilt, and it is common to feel depressed about being depressed. Too often we are left alone without help, or we seek help that impedes. Other major negative forces include peer pressure to take drugs or to indulge in sex. More socially sanctioned obstacles include escaping into marriage and/or becoming overly busy.

Spiritual growth, which includes pain and joy, simply is not congruent with many cultural norms. Young people are expected to be vital and "happy," without a care in the world. To feel loneliness as a prelude to deeper love is seldom accepted. To experience depression in the service of fulfillment is rejected; only fulfillment without emptiness is accepted. In many ways, we impede healthy and holy growth when we are seduced by well-intentioned but negative approaches, such as trying to purge ourselves of necessary anxiety and loneliness.

It is prudent to realize, however, that it is rare and perhaps impossible to be without any "demons," that is, forces which militate against health and growth. Rather than trying to kill our demons, we can understand their devious ways and, paradoxically, become stronger. In other words, we combat madness with sanity, and we confront our demons with good spirits. With spiritual help, we descend to the underworld in order to ascend with greater vision and strength. To go with God is important because, when we forget that we are sinners who need to be saved, we risk damnation.

In escaping and transcending negative forces, a good home and an understanding family are important aids. If parents are closed or unavailable, a mature brother or sister, a relative, or a friend can be sought. People who understand and appreciate our worlds can help us lessen the pain and increase the joy of becoming young adults.

Hopefully, religious ministers are available and can respond to our questions. Their purpose is to witness to us and help us in our journey to the Promised Land.

With or without family and friends, a trustworthy mentor usually plays a significant role in young adulthood. Ideally, our primary mentors have been and continue to be our parents. Other mentors such as a teacher, supervisor, counselor, older friend, or relative can influence the way we develop. A good mentor gives witness to holy and healthy attitudes, embodies a wholesome lifestyle, and encourages, supports, and inspires us to become our better selves. Our challenge is to choose and cultivate mentors of the heart as well as of the mind. Academic and professional mentors will guide our intellectual and functional pursuits; spiritual mentors, however, are paramount in the ongoing formation of holiness and happiness. With the help of mentors, we novices of adulthood can learn to become competent and virtuous adults.

In these times of immediate satisfaction, patience is a lost art. As young adults, it is difficult to accept waiting in the desert for the promised land of fulfillment. Instead of going too quickly or experiencing too much too soon, it is better to go slowly. We can take time to explore and experience people, events, and places. Taking time for solitude, as in any life passage, is crucial in coming to discover and be oneself. Reading relevant literature can affirm and clarify the confusion and darkness of self-emergence as well as nurture our searching selves. A personal journal, in which we consider our experiences daily in order to increase our awareness, can also be helpful. The advent of adulthood calls for a prudent and patient journey in faith.

LAND OF SURRENDER

This period of implementation, though not without stress, is a relatively stable and settled time in contrast to the more unsettled desert time. Life usually comes together for better or worse. It is the time to explore and master the world—a time when most of us begin our professional and personal vocations. Although these decisions are not irrevocable, they make a significant impact on our future lives.

Along with external exploration, we learn to be "normative adults," partly because of social responsibilities, career expectations, and pressure to function successfully. As young adults, we are expected to learn to adjust to the world and learn to implement the roles of worker, player, citizen, socializer, individual, community member, spouse, parent, helper, and friend.

Young adulthood is the time when we are challenged to live commitments and values that shape our lives, and the way we implement them depends highly on our desert experiences. If we circumvent the desert, we can easily become overinvolved with social and economic responsibilities and forget to nourish our spiritual selves. A common error that militates against spiritual growth is to measure our worth by our material possessions and social status. Climbing up the economic and social ladder may well mean a diminution of spirituality. It is easy to be seduced by a madness that minimizes and rationalizes spiritual living.

Communal living is a strong test of our commitment and values. For example, a strong or weak marital foundation is usually built in young adulthood. The prudent young couple realizes that they must consistently practice a virtuous life; otherwise, they can simply adjust and forget to love. Other realities such as children, work, and financial problems also challenge us. Members of a religious community and clerics soon learn the difference between their "spiritual honeymoon" and the humdrum of everyday living. Living a healthy communal life while being single is perhaps the most difficult challenge of all.

Living in love is a concrete test of integrating that which is functional and that which is spiritual. Ideally, we begin to practice unconditional love, that is, learning to love without expectation of or need for return. We begin to learn that love is not primarily a matter of satisfying our needs. How to cultivate living in love is a key factor in developing a spiritual life. There is a danger of becoming too absorbed with the functional grind of living and neglecting one's spiritual core, or becoming codependent in taking responsibility for others' well-being while forgetting one's own welfare. How we begin this journey of love significantly impacts the rest of our lives.

Friendship can also be an important element of spiritual growth. To be understood and appreciated in more than functional ways can give needed courage to pursue the spiritual life. Such friendship can help us to accept and transcend the problems that inevitably evolve in living spiritually. It can also give us support and help to nourish our spiritual selves at a time that demands that we be highly functional.

As young adults, we can deceive ourselves by assuming that we have plenty of time to change our lives. We may live as if we have innumerable possibilities to do what we want. Living in the illusion of inexhaustible time, we can take life and love for granted. In our naive optimism, we can forget to nourish our spiritual lives. As "free spirits" we can fail to develop structures for our growth in freedom. Consequently, we can slowly and unknowingly lose our spirits.

Toward the end of young adulthood, we can probably look back on milestones such as personal vocation, parenthood, and career choice. These kinds of milestones are important and the challenge is to integrate them with our spiritual lives. Thus, it behooves us to promote the interior life. Instead of being too outer-directed, we can be vigilant in setting structures that foster spiritual growth. Rather than succumbing to social and cultural pressure, to value having over being and function over spirit, life can center on becoming primarily and ultimately spiritual.

Without spiritual values, life slowly becomes a sham and a hell. Forgetting the Spirit of Life blinds us to beautiful visions and silences mystical music. It stops joyful rhythms, suppresses pleasant aromas, blunts delectable tastes, and aborts peaceful rest. It is practical and life-giving to savor the Spirit.

Chapter 7

Established Adulthood

By the end of our third decade, most of us have learned to cope with the demands, responsibilities, and overall vicissitudes of living as well as having gained some satisfaction and success. But just when life seems set, we begin to look again at the past and wonder about the future. We get the uncomfortable feeling that our comfort will soon end, for a new desert appears on the horizon.

As in earlier transitions, we experience new expectations from ourselves and others. We feel the pressure to "act adult"—to be sober, settled, and sane. No longer do we have quite the same freedom to be silly, unsettled, or "young." At work or play, we strongly feel the need to be responsible and "older." Our transition from young adulthood ushers in the desert of established adulthood.

Though we may have been aware of becoming older, we feel our age in new and uneasy ways. Reaching the age of twenty-nine, we are aware of youth slipping away. We are pressured to admit that soon we will no longer be young, but rather "mature." We are people who are neither young nor old and not yet in the middle years, but people who have been seasoned. Unsettling as it may be, we are faced with the fact that the last vestiges of youth have slipped away.

DESERT OF SELF-CONCERN

Questions! Questions! Questions! Just when life was becoming orderly, something again unsettles it. After the busy years of establishing ourselves in the adult world, a new desert may come as a surprise or seem unfair. We may feel that we should be settled by now; nevertheless, we again question life. What's it all about? Who have I become? Do I want the next ten years to be like the past ten? What about me? What are my goals? What are my values? Am I living the way I want to? What is best for me? What about me? Is this all there is ? In short: the focus is on "me."

Our primary concern is for our own welfare. Although there is a peril of egotism and excessive self-centeredness that is to be avoided, a proper respect for oneself as well as for others is necessary and healthy. Rather than being an exercise in narcissism, our desert of self-concern is a necessary part of spiritual growth. A main task is to claim our freedom—freedom *from* and freedom *for*. In this desert, we focus on what life can give us and on what we can freely give in return.

More questions: How am I physically? How do I look? How do I want to look? How do I dress? Do I dress as a young person? As an older person? What does it mean to look physically mature? While feeling the tug of aging and its impending limits, we may try harder than ever to prove ourselves physically in an attempt to hold on to youth. Though in "good shape," we feel the pressure to work at staying in "good shape" because feeling out of shape can be an unsettling affirmation of getting older.

We also become concerned about our personal commitments. Is marriage as good as we initially thought it would be? Too often, we find that it has dissipated rather than grown. We question our past motives: Why did I get married? Did I marry the right person? Do I still really love? What is happening to my love? Why do you love me? Who loves me? In the midst of such disruption, we may think of changing our commitment. Divorce, or preparing for it, is common at this time. We may also think of ways to renew and to promote marital commitment. If single, we can be pressured to get married or can be patronized, pitied, or subtly rejected. If we are a member of a community, we may feel that this is the time to leave or to renew our commitment.

Some women intensely feel the impoverishment of their lives. They feel they give love much more than they receive it. Women who are taken for granted and sold short can feel alone and lonely even in a busy house. Many begin to protest and demand more appreciation and love.

Frequently, for example, women protest against being treated mainly as a function—mother, wife, provider, worker, servant, and "second-class citizen." A woman might say: "I am tired of being a servant, of giving, giving, giving. I've worked for ten years without pay or much recognition. And, I've worked for pay, though for less than my male counterparts. Nevertheless, my family simply expects me to be always available to wait on them. I'm tired of being taken for granted. What about me? Who gives to me? I want more! I am more!"

Many men are so involved in their work that they can easily make their personal commitments secondary to their jobs. A wife, then, is secondary and marriage adjusts to mediocrity. Since a man's self-concern is more likely to be channeled in work or recreational activities, personal loneliness and the desire to grow in love are not often clearly and strongly felt. Unfortunately, many men minimize interpersonal growth and settle for functional contentment. Some men do listen to their spirit that yearns for more than comfort and success.

It is no surprise, therefore, that this time is prime for divorce. Many couples covertly agree to an implicit divorce: to adjust (for the sake of children, economic security, or social conveniences) to a merely functional, although dying, marriage. A divorce in midlife or middle age is often decided ten or twenty years before. Our challenge is to listen to and act upon the call to deepen the marital commitment, that is, to foster communication (the mind of marriage) and to foster love (the heart of marriage).

Single persons, particularly women, usually suffer the oppression of diminishing opportunities for marriage. Women often experience sexist and ageist prejudices that impede their free movement in pursuing a marital commitment. The ugly probability is that a mature woman in her thirties will encounter few mature men eligible for marriage. To compound the situation, many men, both single and married, consider single women as lonely and desperate sex objects who can be easily exploited.

Thus, single women who seek to be mature and who want to grow spiritually find it difficult at this time because of prejudice against their age, sex, and maturity. A sad irony is that most women are reaching their psychological and sexual peak at thirty so that, in many ways, they are more than ever ready to be married. At the same time, many courageous women have deepened their spiritual lives to a degree that intimidates many men.

We also wonder about the relevance of our work. Unpaid workers, such as homemakers, may question the worth of their work. This is understandable in light of society's tendency to judge the value of work according to financial and power criteria. We can assume that more pay means more valuable work. It is easy to doubt the worth of unpaid work in the midst of a materialistic culture.

We might ask ourselves if our careers and spiritual lives work in harmony. Does work impede or implement our spiritual values? Are our spiritual lives more important than our functional lives? Are our lives primarily involved in service so that spirituality is secondary? Do we slavishly listen to the tick of "clock time" while being deaf to the kairotic time of love? Are our lives so scheduled that we have little time for God? Are we so busy being useful that we are too tired to be "uselessly" present at more permanent and life-giving experiences? Can we foster experiences that are ends in themselves rather than means to other ends? Are we so intent on achieving that we lack the patience to wait for God?

It is difficult to respond authentically to such questions. Increased financial and career pressures can insidiously trap us into being dedicated workaholics. Too tired to play, too preoccupied to relax, or just a general feeling of being on a treadmill are symptoms of maximizing work and minimizing spirituality. In the desert of adulthood, we are pressured to take stock of what meaning our work has and can have.

Social roles and environmental structures are also examined. For example, a woman asks what it means to be a wife, mother, and woman; a man questions the meaning of being a husband, father, and man. A woman at this time is especially sensitive to the problems and possibilities of role functioning. She becomes concerned about herself and her future in contrast to exclusively serving others. A married woman may feel irritated with social activities and friends that are primarily oriented around her children and husband. Feeling trapped in a social desert may evoke an urge to "get out." Whatever the situation, women who become aware of their environmental restrictions and possibilities often strive to move from oppression to self-determination.

In the struggle to be freer, there is a danger of minimizing spiritual power and maximizing social and political power. A challenge, particularly for women, is to strive for equal opportunity and just treatment while deepening and nourishing their spiritual lives. This then becomes a permanent and powerful ground on which to stand and act. Otherwise, women become just as "mad" as many men in their pursuit of economic and political power.

It is even easier for men to forget their spiritual selves. The pressure to achieve "male goals" that bring economic and social success can easily militate against spiritual living. To go beyond the false image of manhood and to maintain and foster spirituality, in the midst of secular society, takes considerable vision, courage, and support. To be a sanctuary and ambassador of Spirit is not common.

Contrary to popular belief, at this time in life, many women surpass men in genital sexuality. Women begin to peak genitally in their thirties while most men decline. Thus, a husband and wife may be moving in opposite directions. When a woman desires more than a man can or wants to give, she can intimidate him, particularly if she integrates her genital needs with her spiritual life. In defense, a man might cover his fear with "quick" sexual exercises according to his desire and convenience. He might rationalize his changing behavior by saying that he is overworked, too tired, or not in the mood.

Furthermore, we have seen that women are usually more open to affective sexuality both as an end in itself and as a means to genital sex, while men tend to view affection mainly as a means to genital gratification. Expressions of affection can threaten men who experience it as necessarily linked to genital sex. Feeling that they must perform genitally whenever they are intimate, men may begin to build the foundation for midlife impotence.

Unlike women, most men have difficulty in being physically intimate without feeling pressured to engage in genital intercourse. One response is to withdraw from intimate relationships and compensate with functional ones. Consequently, intimacy—the linkage of souls—suffers and withers. Women's openness to affective intimacy as an end in itself nourishes intimacy while men's tendency to bind affection with genitality impedes their intimacy. Women are less likely than men to fragment sexuality and less likely to settle for less than is really possible—whole sex.

Adult women, however, can easily be frustrated in both the sexual and spiritual realms, and intimacy can wane and be forgotten. If a woman is frustrated, the time is ripe for an affair. She is young enough to be "considered attractive," has the know-how to get around, and often has more opportunity. Addictive and coaddictive behaviors are also common responses to such frustration. Such behaviors are human and understandable, but ineffective and harmful.

A recurrent danger is to become so busy that we forget what is essential for health. For example, a person may be actively involved in religion and still fail to promote spiritual growth. Often a well-intentioned life of social service displaces or impedes a direct and active spiritual life. Solitude, creative pauses, and prayer are neglected or dissociated from the rest of life so that spiritual experiences may be felt as distant or as a thing of the past. To hear the call of spirituality in a loud and busy world is difficult. The desert pressures us to slow down, to be patient in an impatient world, and to silence words in order to listen to the Word of God.

Our moral systems, whatever they are, are challenged. In our thirties, we are usually responsible for influencing the moral development of children, while most of us are questioning our own moral standards. "Superego-less" adults, who have become morally indifferent, wonder about what is best for themselves and others. Some develop an expedient moral system based on self-satisfaction, and others have a rigid moral system that is equally self-centered. This is a time to deepen our spiritual foundations and grow in moral maturity.

In the desert of established adulthood, single people especially feel the pain of loneliness and isolation. Although they may have social freedom, many lack a consistent reference group, so that they often feel like outsiders. To compound matters, to be single in one's thirties evokes overconcern or prejudgments. Judgmental statements are heard: "Isn't it too bad they are single? Are they homosexual? What's wrong with him? What's going to happen to her?" Besides being lonely, single people are often oppressed, exploited, rejected, pitied, or merely tolerated.

Being single, especially female, often means exclusion from social functions, or, at best, only being tolerated. To be one of a pair is the membership card needed to enter many social functions with approval. Finding that roads, telephone lines, and invitations travel one way, singles can get discouraged trying to get "in." Some look for singles groups that foster social activities, but seldom for those which foster spiritual life. In some of these groups, women can be seen as commodities to be used. Although being used or filling up time can seem better than nothing, such spiritless activity soon becomes boring and empty.

Some celibates seek to build friendships as a way of responding to loneliness. Others cope with loneliness by being so busy that they have no time to listen. Some use sex and/or alcohol to numb the sting of loneliness. Yet, our primary goal is not to escape loneliness, but rather to listen to it and respond to this call to love ourselves and others, to receive love, and to seek love ultimately from God.

Yet love is not always easy. Sometimes it is present in absence and we question it. Where and how and with whom do I want to live a life of love? Is it possible to be intimate forever? Can I love? Who? How? Am I loved? Though love is challenged, we are simultaneously pressured to escape from these important questions of intimacy—of interpersonal spirituality. It is easy to become so busy that we forget to renew life. When we do not deepen our love, we increase loneliness and build the foundation for a dreadfully painful midlife crisis.

A dangerous assumption with respect to loneliness is that people can ultimately satisfy their own spiritual needs. The reality is that only God can ultimately respond to our radical call of love. Only God's Spirit can support and give us life permanently and everywhere. Only God is our common ground. Loneliness is a living reminder that we are primarily dependent on God, not on one another. Indeed, we depend on one another in many ways, but such interdependency is secondary to our primary dependency on God.

In our desert thirties, we begin to realize that the absence in loneliness seems to be a more permanent presence. We come to realize in absence, God is more present. Since spiritual loneliness first seeks God and others, interpersonal and community relationships are precariously tenuous and they progressively dissipate in

Spirit when God is forgotten. Grounded together in God, however, we can courageously strive to love unrestrictedly.

Likewise, the emptiness of spiritual depression can only be fulfilled by God. Its heavy listlessness can only be enlightened and vitalized by the Holy Spirit. Social success, economic possession, political power, and psychological insight will not heal the depressed spirit. Though medical and psychosocial approaches can and should be used to treat medical and psychosocial depressions, these methods are inadequate for spiritual experiences. Sometimes tranquilizing and analyzing hinder the emergence of spiritual questions that seek transcendent answers.

Rather than whispering its message as in young adulthood, death speaks more clearly: Live! Yet, many studies affirm how we, in this culture, seek to escape death and dying. This is tragic, for facing death is our saving grace. Coming to terms with death can evoke a sense of wonder that helps us take a second look at life. When we ask the question, "Is this all there is?" we can answer, "No. There is infinitely more!" We begin to sense that learning how to live freely and serenely has much to do with learning how to listen to the voice of death.

In this desert of nothingness, death proclaims our radical powerlessness—life is not totally or even primarily in our hands. We start to realize that we cannot really control anyone and that self-control is limited. Often, in the midst of the thriving thirties, we come to accept our powerlessness and come to believe that only a Higher Power/Care can save us from our illusion of power. Paradoxically, accepting our powerlessness *empowers* us.

One of the strongest desert demons will tempt us with hyperactivity. Too often, we fail to slow down, rest, play, or celebrate. We desperately try to find the meaning of life in what we do rather than in who we are. Consequently, we seldom take time to celebrate the mystery of being alive and, when we do have time, we become frightened and anxious. Holidays become so hectic that we are glad when they are over. We become obsessed with activity and life becomes a matter of adjusting to, and coping with, an unending series of demands. We can be programmed to strive for mere achievement and fall far short of integral serenity. Such false promises of happiness result in controlled despair. Relatively early in life, when we still have many years to live, we already feel weary and discouraged. Celebration and enjoyment of life have been crowded out.

To tame these desert demons and promote spiritual growth, particularly at this time, we can take creative pauses to listen to and reflect on our lives. It helps to take stock of our interpersonal spirituality. How is a life of love really lived? How can it be improved? The desert is an opportune place to listen to the summons of loneliness: to love.

In the desert, we are less likely to be hyperactive and more likely to take time to slow down to listen to our reason for being. We can reflect on how to practice the daily art of loving. We can think of ways to structure our time and space for genuine play rather than workaholism, for community rather than depending on self-sufficiency, for passionate growth rather than continued adjustment, and for a life with the Holy Spirit rather than a life of living vicariously.

LAND OF SELF-ACTUALIZATION

The rhythm of differentiation and integration, of darkness and light, and of death and life goes on perpetually. For better and/or worse, most adults come out of the desert more seasoned and settled. The decade of the thirties is often a settling time to become one's stable self.

Most of us acquire more power and responsibility along with a desire to make a mark on the world. Psychosocially, it is a time to increase and focus our efforts on succeeding personally and professionally. It is a busy and stressful time when we strive to make things happen at work, in social interactions, and in our personal lives. In our thirties, we continue to "go out" to establish ourselves. We should enjoy and meet the challenges of this time, for soon our exterior journeys will begin to be more interior journeys.

By now, we have solidified the decisions that highly influence our present and future functional and personal lives. Many married women have taken a new stand toward their domestic responsibilities. Some get involved in social and political activities, religious functions, or educational pursuits. Those who do not join a group or engage in an "outside" activity are still likely to explore their "inner" freedom by reading and personal reflection. Some women repress their awareness and adjust to frustrating and fragmented lives.

Unfortunately, too many of us have learned to adjust to a life with minimal spirit. The thriving thirties can result in a mad adjustment to a spiritless life. Rather than a time to fall out of love, it is a time to share equally, to accept limits in ourselves and others, and to strengthen our bonds with one another. We can learn to accept, manage, and celebrate our being in a perpetually problematic community.

When we build our lives around values that foster virtue, our lives change. Rather than choosing friends who are only useful for professional and social success, we spend more time in fellowship that nurtures us spiritually. Instead of withdrawing from our spouses, we become closer by reaffirming and deepening our primary commitment. Paradoxically, our desert concern for ourselves leads to concern for others. Such self-actualization incorporates others.

In healthy relationships, we share ourselves with mutual respect. As we learn from and enjoy one another, we begin to feel freer to take on the attributes of the other sex. Women, in particular, assert their spirits, tolerate less oppression, and pursue a freer and more integral life. Men, however, too often become slaves to work and the pursuit of success, and their spirits become contained and passionless.

Instead of being a frantic time of activism and workaholism, established adulthood can be an optimum time for play. For most of us, it is the last time for boundless physical energy and vigor. We may be still near our physical peak so that we can engage in vigorous activities. Furthermore, we have the know-how and desire to play with zest and freedom. Our challenge is not to overlook, but to respond to life as a free banquet for feasting.

If we have not resolved our crises positively, we can continue to escape spiritual growth especially in overactivity such as workaholism and compensatory pleasure. We run from death, for we construe death as the opposite of life and as total absurdity. Rather than evoking life, death promises annihilation.

If this desert journey leads to a positive resolution, we are renewed in the Spirit of Life. Death is not denied but is accepted and listened to as a source of life. It behooves us to take time out to listen and to reflect on death—our own and that of others.

Listening to our own deaths enables us to listen to the death of others and, consequently, appreciate their lives more. For example, knowing that living brings us closer to death, we can appreciate our parents' approaching death, and take measures to enjoy them more than ever. Being in touch with our being-toward-death helps us to slow down and to take time to savor life so that its spirit does not pass us by.

Creative pauses, solitude, reflective reading, enjoyment, prayer, humor, and intimacy are ways to combat the many obstacles to growth as well as maintaining and nurturing ourselves. We must take time to see and listen to the beauty of life and its people. Rather than forgetting the heart of life, we can be vigilant in guarding and proclaiming life's Spirit. Then this promised land of established adulthood is a good place to be—for awhile.

Chapter 8

Midlife Adulthood

Midlife adulthood has been a popular topic. Considerable research from both stage (organismic) and nonstage (environmental) perspectives has increased our understanding of this period of adult development. Most studies, however, have focused on the physical, psychological, and social dimensions of midlife development, while little attention has been given to its spiritual dimension. Our approach is to focus on midlife spiritual development.

In our schema, midlife is the time between established adulthood and middle age, or generally between ages thirty-nine and forty-nine. Again, the age range is given to locate and concretize a period of development that usually differs from other periods. Although in midlife we are not yet middle-aged, we are probably approaching the halfway point of our life expectancy. At times, we realize that we may have less time to live than we have already lived.

As we approach forty, we look back. We may feel a peculiar discomfort in acknowledging that high school graduation occurred more than twenty years ago. We begin to reflect on our past dreams, goals, and ideals. Have they been fulfilled or unfulfilled? We question again. Have my personal and professional goals been reached? Have I truly lived according to my values and ideals? Have I grown? Am I growing? Have I made a significant contribution to life? Have I stopped dreaming?

Whatever our previous doubts about reaching adulthood, at forty there is no doubt about it. Most of us find that we are slowing down and feeling less energetic than in the past. Keeping in shape, for example, may be more work than play. Since we already have many personal and social responsibilities, we are reluctant to commit time and energy to enter a new time of transition and trial. The promise of change threatens our lifestyles and some of us prefer to stay at thirty-nine, or regress to twenty-nine or nineteen.

At the threshold of this desert, we can hear the faint but clear voice of the noonday devil. Death can be seen lurking in the distant shadows, seeking a confrontation, perhaps mocking us, and trying to intimidate us so we withdraw from the desert. Now is the time we need courage to enter the desert, faith to face and transcend our limited selves, and hope to answer the demon of death with life.

DESERT OF LIMITS

Nothingness again embraces us. We see nothing. We hear nothing. We feel nothing. We wonder what is happening to our recently clear and ordered life when things seemed to be working out. Now, we feel so different: Will anything work out? So what if it does?

The midlife desert is permeated with the dreadful and redeeming experience of limits. Initially, we experience the limits of our physical selves. It is easy to be out of physical shape at this age, and we may feel helpless in getting back into shape. Many of us have more ailments than we have previously had and, since we are likely to become more aware of harmful practices that affect our physical welfare, we may begin to implement programs to improve ourselves. We may stop smoking and drinking, or begin dieting and exercising. In general, we feel pressured to care more about our health.

Not infrequently, we first become aware of our psychospiritual changes by their physical manifestation. Fatigue, weakness, tension, and depression are indications that something has happened and is happening. Such experiences speak to us, and we can listen to them. Weariness may mean that we have been overactive. Tension and anxiety may be telling us that we are overextended and fragmented. Depression may be saying that we have lost our spirit in our frenetic pursuit to "make it." The limits of our physical selves may be telling us to seek more than the limited.

Although we are likely to have more psychological knowledge and better coping mechanisms, we nevertheless experience the limits of how we manage and succeed. We become disillusioned with the popular assumption that happiness is a function of success and psychological well-being. Though we may have learned to function well, to think clearly, to speak effectively, and to act appropriately, we feel out of it. We feel confused about "it"—about what is missing. Feeling the limits of our past ways, we are called to face our foolish selves, to laugh at the noonday devil, to seek something more, and to be enlightened in and with the Transcendent.

A particularly painful, but redeeming, experience is to be confronted with our deceptive and foolish selves. The midlife desert is the place where we are unveiled, demasked, and exposed. We come face-to-face with the ways we have deceived ourselves and others. It is the time when we are pressured to realize how we did not live according to the values we professed, how we said one thing and did another, and how we convinced ourselves to believe what isn't so.

The midlife desert angels pressure us to see more truthfully and to be better. But, we can deceive ourselves in many ways, often with sincere and good intentions. For example, some couples pretend to be happily married while they deny their unhappiness. Some religious and ministers sincerely exhibit one lifestyle in public and quite another in private. Many of us seek spiritual meaning while striving for inordinate pleasure and success. Our repressed and rationalized truth demands examination. Do we discern our foolish selves and become wise, or do we prepare to die as fools?

There are many ways to respond to this opportunity of self-disclosure. For example, in seeing ourselves in terms of limits, we can lose perspective on past accomplishments and future possibilities, and become hypercritical of ourselves. We can become depressed because we see ourselves as helpless and empty. Some highly successful men who wield tremendous power feel powerless with the experience of "nothing." Instead of admitting to and letting go of their powerlessness and looking for and responding to the Spirit of Unlimited Power, they escape to the limited worlds of work, addictions, and social power.

Others try to regress to youth, when limits were really not such an issue. For example, in a futile attempt to escape limits, a man has an affair with a younger woman. Part of this normal madness is that it is much easier to have an affair with a young woman who may affirm his illusion of being young than to maintain an ongoing relationship with a woman his own age. Men who are intimidated by a mature woman may engage a less threatening young adult while trying to regain youthful identity.

Midlife can also be a time when latent and unresolved adolescent problems emerge to confuse and scare us. Although we often assume that adolescent experiences are gone forever, the truth is that both positive and negative experiences from the past continue to have an impact on us. Thus, we can be startled with old or "seemingly new" feelings that are reminiscent of adolescence. For instance, if we never resolved adolescent issues such as inferiority, anger, or sexuality, we may be confronted again with these issues. Trying to escape the inevitable crises of limits, we construct a personal tale of being immortal and of thinking that everything is possible. In the midlife desert, we are called finally to give up the ways of a child and take on those of an adult.

If we fail to cope with the desert of midlife, we lose a great opportunity to grow spiritually. That failure may result in psychosomatic illness as well as more debilitating depression and anxiety. For example, high blood pressure, ulcers, headaches, fatigue, or other such afflictions can be the result of impeded spiritual growth.

The healthy and holy response to the midlife crisis is to leap in faith to the Uncreated Spirit of Unlimited Love. By facing our self-deception and accepting our limits, we begin to affirm our ultimate dependence on God. Our loss of control motivates us to surrender our will and life to a greater will and power. When our powerlessness is bonded with a greater power, we become stronger and freer.

Our experience of ourselves, others, and life itself as limited leaves us in a vacuum that draws us to the Unlimited. We let go of our grasp of things and surrender to nothingness. In nothingness, we seek being, and paradoxically find being in nothingness. In our experience of absence, we discover presence. Instead of depending exclusively on the limited (services, possessions, or even other human beings), we surrender to the Unlimited. Depending ultimately on nothing but God, we tap an unlimited source of healing Power.

Another confrontation with life's limits involves a new experience of time. We have the uncomfortable feeling that time is running out. The common phrase "time flies" becomes personally threatening when we clearly hear the loud tick of the clock winding down. We feel vulnerable to time and feel there is nothing much we can do to slow it down. Especially if time is only seen chronologically, it seems to be dreadfully beyond our control. We may ask: What is time? How does time affect me? Where has time gone? What have I done with time? How much time is there? What am I going to do with the time I have left? What will happen in time? When will I die?

Recognizing that everything takes time pressures us to reevaluate our investment of time. Wherever we go and whatever we do takes time; to do one thing takes time away from other possible experiences. Experiencing the limits of time throws us back on ourselves to question where and how time can be experienced best, and ultimately what we will do with the rest of our time.

We are called to transcend the limits of chronological "clock time," to experience kairotic time in its unlimited dimensions. We are challenged to have better times than ever before—to foster and enjoy times of the Spirit. Rather than living primarily according to a schedule, we can orient our life primarily around spiritual times. With patience and vigilance, we prepare to respond to gifted moments of the Spirit.

We discover that there is a time to listen and a time to speak, a time to fast and a time to feast, a time to mourn and a time to rejoice, a time to walk and a time to run, a time to laugh and a time to cry, a time to see and a time to be blind, a time to journey in the desert and a time to travel in the Promised Land, a time to live and a time to die.

In midlife, we are pressured to go beyond the immediate to the "more than," precisely while experiencing the apparent absence of Spirit. In our emptiness, we desire to be fulfilled; in our sense of being lost, we want to find our way. We can experience in our limits an arid absence that calls for a refreshing presence. For some of us, our ground is shaken and perhaps undermined, leaving us scared and wounded. When we gently embrace our broken selves, we begin to heal. When we can ask to be healed, our request is always answered in time.

Spirituality becomes even more of an issue in midlife than in previous times. The call to the interior life is greater and clearer, but unfortunately it can be misinterpreted. We can reject the beckoning of the Spirit, numb the pain of self-emergence, or simply obscure the good news. To become a full-blown workaholic, to regress, to overeat and overdrink, and to repress our spirits are modes of normal madness that violate spiritual growth. They are mad ways because we harm ourselves and miss the ultimate and redemptive meaning of life.

We have seen that, in the desert, we can feel as though we are in a barren land with no one around but ourselves. Can this desert lead to a land of love? Can we move from alienation to compassion, or do we seek to escape from community? Does resentment emerge, grow, and devour us instead of unconditional acceptance of ourselves and others? Do we hear and respond to the silent word of God? Can we learn concretely the meaning of the paschal mystery—the redemptive good of suffering in love for our welfare?

We can also feel boxed in by our personal and professional commitments, feeling subjugated to and overstructured by them. Rather than life-giving, our commitments seem to impede life. Should we continue to live for the next ten or twenty years the way we have been, or should we change? If so, how? We know that change in personal and professional commitments is difficult at midlife. Yet, if we have been deceiving ourselves, our limits call for change. If personal commitment has been based only on convenience or on mere functionality, our relationships have seriously dissipated by now and our spirits cry for "more than" has been. We must admit to our charades of commitment and pretending to grow together in love. Sharing our weakness with God and trustworthy people can enable us to come to reconciliation, make creative restitution, and restructure our lives for the better.

The desert offers another redemptive experience: to allow repressed feelings to emerge. For example, a married couple who have repressed anger and resentment for fifteen or more years can suddenly see their marriage as totally negative. They see in each other no positive value, and each resents any happiness the other shows. They may have been afraid to share their hurt and anger, or they simply never learned how to share. Although they may have treated each other decently, they did not grow much in communication and love. Now, the price of their collusion is thrust upon them.

They will do well to face their crisis, grow from it, and then decide to stay with or leave each other.

Men and women often experience midlife differently. Many men desire to retrieve their lost youth because they fear growing older. Sexist pressure moves many men to identify youth with physical virility. Consequently, many men at forty try to manifest a "new life" that resembles the vigor of youth. Jogging, partying, travel, and generally new recreational behavior emerge. Although some women may also regress in response to growing older, others are likely to respond to their limits and pain more maturely.

Furthermore, many women get a second wind that enables them to cope effectively with limits, especially women who have dealt well with their earlier desert experiences. They often feel determined to improve and to explore, relying on their inner resources more than on external activities. Rather than needing people or circumstances to change, they change what they can—themselves.

A common and dangerous reaction to the midlife limits of intimacy is to expect others—parents, spouse, friends, relatives—to be the primary source of love. Such a reaction is understandable but futile. Indeed, as children we all appropriately depend on particular people for our well-being. But as adults we are called to go beyond our childhood ways and learn to care, with God, for ourselves. No human can love perpetually without restriction. To depend primarily and ultimately on any one individual for love is unrealistic, for only God is the unlimited and omnipresent source of love. God, and no one else, is our saving grace.

The desert proclaims that, when we need any "one" except God to be our primary sustenance, we make that person a god. We can put people on pedestals and bind them to us as perfect ideals. We subtly and unconsciously manipulate them to act the way we feel they should. Soon they feel pressured to conform to our expectations and, consequently, they feel frustrated, angry, and resentful.

To be sure, we need people to love and we need them to love us. We are called to love one another and to form and nurture a community of love with its consequent freedom and serenity. To give and receive love from ourselves, others, and God is necessary for holiness and healthiness, but to need love (or anything) from a particular human being, from any "one," is immature. Such a dependent, codependent, or addictive approach risks displacing God as the only One who can give us sanity and sanctity.

Thus, we need love from God and want love from others. Our challenge is to love others and want (rather than need) them to love us. Ideally, we love unconditionally, that is, without the condition of our needs being satisfied. Bonding with God helps us to accept and manage when our love is not returned or when it is violated.

Intimacy is rooted in the Spirit of God-others-self, with God being our life-giving Source. Being grounded in this primary Source of Life motivates us to strive to love unconditionally—to manifest God. Rooted in inexhaustible love, we have the courage to risk in love and the strength to accept rejection, which is a challenging test of love. When we consistently practice inner bonding with God-others-self, we need nothing from anyone and can better accept and manage what we cannot change. Our divine dependency enables us to love and to be loved unconditionally—the basis of intimacy, freedom, and serenity. The desert is a prime place to learn the limits of exclusively human love and to encounter the unlimited care and power of God's Love.

In midlife, death comes out of the shadows and manifests itself. Rather than whispering its message, death speaks clearly and loudly. Rather than knocking at our door, death opens our door and greets us. Death demands to be heard: Can you transcend your culture that denies death? Can you really face and listen to me? Can you admit your ultimate powerlessness? Can you escape me—the ultimate limit? Can you live forever?

Aging makes it increasingly difficult to silence our wake-up call. Still, we can deny our being-toward-death so that, rather than evoking life, death promises annihilation. Death becomes the opposite of life. It is total absurdity and life becomes a frantic, fruitless attempt to escape death and, therefore, authentic living.

Along with confronting our own dying, the death of grandparents and perhaps parents is also likely to occur at this time. The death and impending death of others throws us back on ourselves, asking us to reevaluate life. Accepting our own being-toward-death and recognizing our powerlessness to do anything about it can lead us to transcend death—to surrender to the ultimate Unlimited who conquers the ultimate limit. Paradoxically, acceptance of our radical powerlessness as it is clearly manifested in death leads to infinite power.

A common temptation, in the midlife desert, is to demonize ourselves. In focusing too much on limits, we can lose perspective and try to escape into conventional modes of fulfillment, such as workaholism, regression, drugs, or other ineffective coping strategies. Such reactions are often based on the assumption that happiness excludes limits and pain, and that life should be perfect and perpetual pleasure. To compound matters, people offer little or no compassionate counsel. We can easily feel inadequate in knowing what to do and guilty for having such feelings.

Efforts to purge and treat our limits, rather than accept and go beyond them, also impede our growth. To be limited, to feel pain, and to be in darkness are frowned upon. Health professions offer biochemistry and psychotherapy to change us. Our experience is usually interpreted as symptomatic of possible pathology or, at least, something to purge. Such attempts to "do" something silence our spiritual questions. We can find it very difficult to respond to the challenge of midlife—to transcend to the Unlimited. How does it happen?

Unlike many physical and functional activities, we cannot *make* it happen. Nevertheless, although spirituality is beyond our control, we are not helpless. We can take measures *(chronos)* to increase the likelihood of spiritual experiences *(kairos)*. First of all, we can abstain from displacements of spirituality, such as addictions, coaddictions, and negative coping. Then, we can reflect on how to avail ourselves to the Transcendent.

We can seek support and help if we need it, and all of us need it. To share with a spouse, friend, mentor, or director, to read spiritual books and journals, and to be a participant in a spiritual fellowship are all beneficial. Staying in shape physically, psychologically, and spiritually also engender availability. To play, sing, dance, minister, be quiet, and sit still open us to God's presence. To be mindful of God's presence in everyday life also increases our awareness. We can let go (of control) and let God make a difference.

We have seen that many midlife issues center on the experience of limits. As these limits enclose us, they challenge us to seek deeper dimensions in life. Instead of evoking denial, projection, depression, regression, or escapism, the experience of limits is an opportunity to encounter the Unlimited. Neither to identify with limits nor to demonize ourselves, but rather to accept our limits and foster our radical dependency on God are paramount. As the finitude of time calls forth the timeless, so the ultimate limit—death—renews life and generates the Infinite—our Spirit who is God.

The midlife desert can be a time to move deeper into hell or into heaven. It can be an exercise in frantic futility or growth in enthusiastic living. It can be a time to face our foolish selves and become our integral selves, or it can be a time to dissipate physically, to be burdened psychologically, and to forget the spiritual life. In either case, healthy or mad, the transition passes and implementation begins.

LAND OF UNLIMITEDNESS

In our forties, we usually experience relatively less stress and more realistic expectations of and from ourselves and others. Some of us learn to accept our limits, which serve as a springboard to the Unlimited, or we try to deny or escape from them and become more limited. Some of us have faced our demonic selves while others continue to run from their dark sides. In short: rejecting and running from the midlife desert leads to an impotent life. Accepting and learning in the desert brings us closer to the Promised Land of Unlimited Power—Uncreated Love.

When we depend on God, life becomes progressively transcendent. Instead of demanding heaven, we celebrate being on earth, which is the prelude to the kingdom. In accepting life's limits, love grows and we live with more joy and spirit. We become compassionate persons who help and heal. We realize that the commitment to love compassionately is essential precisely because we are limited. Such an open and steadfast love gives us direction and solidarity in living a life that ultimately makes sense.

Accepting the limits of love moves us to foster an unconditional love. However, if we have built up anger and hurt from the past, we are likely to express resentment at this time. We are prone to see others only in terms of their limits instead of embracing their limits in love. Rather than helping them, we retaliate with hostility and fail to grow in love.

If we deny our limits, we may try to become unlimited with hyperactivity or numb the pain of being mortal through drugs. Whatever we do to avoid our limits and the Unlimited, we feel superficially alive. Running from the transcendent life, we feel tired, beaten, and less alive. Simply to exist becomes a heavy effort.

If we opt for the Spirit, we become more spirited and alive. In spite of our lost youth, we become more beautiful because we integrate our physical, psychological, and spiritual dimensions. We accept and understand the stress of a life that leads to death and, rather than depending only on social sciences to save us, we also rely on God. Our limits urge us to surrender to the Source of Life.

In the promised land of midlife, we realize that death and dying can help us live more fully. In facing death, we are more able to help those who mourn the death of loved ones as well as to comfort ourselves in death. We realize that, in certain ways, dead people are more alive in their disembodiment and more present in their absence than in their physical presence. Though we miss them, our loved ones live forever.

It is easy to take growth for granted in relatively settled times, particularly in a culture that does not actively promote and reward spirituality. We can nourish our spiritual lives by reflecting on our recent critical past and by living with a sense of the Unlimited. We can foster a "contemplative disposition" by "seeing" more than is apparent. Experiencing the Unlimited in the midst of daily limits enables us to dance with the Spirit of Life. We celebrate the mystery of living, laugh with life, and live with a divine perspective. We become enthusiastic people living in, through, and with God.

As in the desert, however, we can displace our yearning for spirituality with activities that temporarily satisfy us. Rather than responding authentically to the call of the Spirit, we become displaced persons who are fragmented, lost, and are, ironically, very limited. We lose our original Spirit, which is the love that binds us in community. Without a spiritual vision, we get lost or, at best, try to settle for less than is possible. We live without authentic community and without being together in God's Love.

Sexuality can become better in midlife. We can become true men and women—integral people who feel freer to incorporate the attributes of the other sex. Men, for instance, can become more affectionate and women can become more assertive. Both sexes can feel freer to nurture, assert, give, and receive. We become truly androgynous.

The affective dimension of sexuality can also be better integrated and appreciated. We realize that we can be intimate without genital relations. Men, in particular, can more fully realize the possibilities of affection as a beautiful end in itself. Integrated with spirituality, genitality has more depth, flexibility, and fulfillment. Its consequences linger longer and significantly influence our everyday lives. Thus, men, in particular, need not be less sexual, but rather *more* sexual.

Living spiritually helps us to become more creative, flexible, and productive workers. Instead of work having little meaning or becoming workaholics who make work our god, our work is grounded in, sustained by, and is a manifestation of spirituality. Although we can succeed in work, functional success is not our ultimate value. Work is very important, but it is, at best, uselessly present in the Spirit. To affirm and touch the Spirit become more important than functional service.

Spiritual experiences are gifts for which we make time. When we totally and tightly schedule life, we have no time for the paramount experiences. We miss the permanent and recurrent kairotic times of play, wonder, love, celebration, contemplation, and joy. We must say "no" to some important, but secondary opportunities; otherwise, we become overextended and too busy for more important moments. We are called to structure our lives in ways that invite God's presence.

When we embrace the Spirit within us, everything in life improves, including play. Vacations are not simply a time to recuperate from work, but are chronological opportunities to renew and engender kairotic times. The aesthetic dimension of nature and art also becomes vibrantly real, and enlightens everyday living. We can appreciate Being in anything, particularly in what we are apt to take for granted. The common ground on which all people stand is seen as the Spirit we manifest. Art and architecture, nature, and things used and enjoyed show the glory of God's presence.

We can strive to make the finite infinite. In day-to-day living, we can transcend or look for more than the conventional and, eventually, see more than the ordinary. We can experience what each of us presupposes, that which radically binds us together—the Unlimited Source of Love. We can concretely see Being in beings, Sacred in the profane, and the Unlimited in the limited. Seeing so much, we take a humble stance; we come down to earth in our appreciation of life and celebrate being with one another in the Holy Spirit.

Fostering a contemplative disposition, we can appreciate ourselves as being different colored and sized threads in the same tapestry. Individually, some threads may seem more beautiful and stronger than others. Some threads may look tattered, ugly, and weak but, when woven together, all the threads—we—create a beautiful and strong tapestry. Every thread contributes to the whole. We become a thing of beauty.

Such a vision—that we are all brothers and sisters working, suffering, and celebrating together in love—can be a guiding and consoling force in our lives. Valuing individuality is important and taking care of our individual selves is a basic responsibility. Even more important is for individuals to foster and enjoy community. Rather than focusing primarily on "self" or on "other," the spiritual focus is on "us."

However, our culture and the social sciences proclaim individuality as primary while community (spirituality) is denied or secondary, at best. When we follow the narcissistic messages of individualism, we compete against, exploit for individual gain, and manipulate and violate community. "Me" becomes more important than "we." Conversely, when we follow the compassionate message of community, we respect and help one another. We humbly affirm that every thread of the human tapestry has its unique place in the woven fabric of humanity.

We can slow down to see and respond to the Unlimited in the limited. Changing pace, seeing new landscapes or old landscapes in new ways, and taking a contemplative posture in everyday living are ways to the Spirit. We can take time for kairotic events. To feast on feast days and to celebrate on holy days are ways to remind ourselves of the Unlimited in the limits of everyday living. Paradoxically, in the limits of embodiment, we are invited to dance with the Unlimited Spirit of Love. It is the time.

Chapter 9

Middle-Aged Adulthood

Approaching fifty, we make a transition from midlife to middle age. Far removed from youth and approaching the elder years, we are closer to death than to birth. Although we are likely to live another thirty years or more, there is no doubt that we are closing in on our destiny—death, or eternal life.

Like other transitional phases, entering middle age evokes new role expectations from ourselves and others. Young people treat us differently. We might feel that we are over the hump and on a descending path. Actually coming to middle age can be very difficult for those who escaped from rather than managed and transcended issues such as limits.

Tired of being challenged, we might refuse to enter the desert of middle age. Common physical changes, such as circulatory problems, weight gain, loss or graying of hair, and joint problems can make entering the desert ominous. We can regard it with forboding or we can anticipate it as a challenge. If we have grown through our previous passages, we are likely to take this one as another opportunity for growth.

DESERT OF DEPRESSION

The middle-age desert can be perceived as foreign and destructive, or as familiar and creative land. We can avoid with fear or enter, with courage, this dark desert of enlightenment. If previous desert journeys have made experiences such as depression and death familiar rather than foreign, we are likely to cope with and learn from these dark nights and become more intimate with God.

Physical changes may be the first to be seen and felt even more than in midlife. Usually in their fifties, men experience a decline in strength, endurance, and sexual desire. There are also subtle changes in so-called masculine qualities, such as a higher pitched voice, less facial hair, and wider hips. Not infrequently, men suffer discomfort from such ailments as depression, insomnia, digestive disturbances, joint problems, nervousness, fatigue, irritability, and aches and pains.

The female climacteric changes are usually even more overt and acute than a man's. Menopause, along with other bodily and emotional changes, can compound the stress women feel during this time of transition. Hormonal changes, which result in a generalized atrophy of the reproduction system, may also account for some decline in so-called feminine appearance. Facial hair may become coarser, the voice may deepen, body curves may flatten out, and breasts may appear flabby. Furthermore, discomfort such as hot flashes, sweating, flushes, bodily tingling, weight gain, headaches, fatigue, and nervousness are not rare. What all this means to a woman is highly contingent on how she cares for herself as well as on cultural and environmental attitudes.

There is a danger of conforming to negative expectations. For instance, it is not uncommon for women to fulfill the sexist prophecy that menopause means the end of being a true woman and of an enjoyable sex life. Besides lowering their self-esteem, which can engender depression, women who follow such a false script can become or feel unattractive and insipid; this is just the opposite of what they can be. Men can also be sexist victims by falsely assuming that middle age means a restricted, rather than an expansive, life.

Since being a woman and being feminine are not a function of reproduction, but rather a manifestation of maturity, middle-aged women may continue to intimidate many men. Perhaps that is a reason why many men consider them no longer attractive or as "neuter," in spite of contradictory evidence. Such sexual oppression may be a man's way of hiding from his own insecurity and impotence.

Such physical and psychosocial changes can engender a depression in middle age. As we have already explained in Chapter 3, depression can have many causes. Primarily, its etiology is rooted in a combination of sources: endogenous/organic/biochemical or exogenous/psychogenic/environmental, or both combinations. For example, depression may be rooted in environmental changes. If we have centered our lives exclusively around our families, we may be depressed when the families leave. A woman who derives her personal satisfaction solely from mothering may experience significant loss and consequent depression when her children leave home. Middle-aged couples who have made each other the paramount source of well-being may become clinically depressed when one of them dies.

Some persons with no history of mental illness undergo a middle-age, involutional depression characterized by severe depression, anxiety, insomnia, and frequent guilt and somatic preoccupation. Severe depressions that lead to despair can be primarily biochemical, psychogenic, or both. Menopausal or climacteric hormonal changes can also engender depression, particularly for people who maximize the physical and minimize the spiritual.

Besides these forms of biochemical and psychological depressions, spiritual depression may also emerge. Feeling depressed about nothing in particular, we feel at a loss to say what is going on except that nothing much makes sense. Even though we may have lived meaningful and worthwhile lives, sometimes we feel that our reasons for being have deserted us.

Such desert depression is an opportunity to slow down, to reflect, and to recollect life. In depression, we can listen to the reality that invites us to embrace our radical poverty—a nothingness that affirms our ultimate powerlessness and calls for dependency on God. Going beyond all things, or experiencing nothing, we come closer to the ground out of which all beings emerge and are kept alive. By descending into the dark pit of depression, we can ascend to the light space of enthusiasm.

In the middle-age desert, feelings of guilt and failure are not uncommon. We can feel guilty about acts committed twenty or thirty years ago, or we can feel a sense of failure for missed opportunities. If we are inclined to be compulsive, we may blame ourselves for not perfectly realizing all of our aims and objectives. Life appears irreversible and certain opportunities are irrevocably gone. When referring to the future, we feel that life is shorter than it really is. We feel helpless to change things. Besides, we feel exhausted from trying to do the impossible—control life. The desert lures us to let go of our grasp of things and accept our powerlessness.

Anger and resentment may often surface in the desert. Persistent feelings of indignant disapproval may be due to anger that has built up over the years. If, over many years, we submitted to mistreatment, we may have repressed our pent-up feelings. Now, instead of taking everything, we take nothing. No longer are we going to be used as doormats. At least, we will no longer be lowered and used. We demand recognition. Actually, such resentment is often our covert attempt to affirm our dignity.

In a similar way, if we have been dependent most of our lives, we may become independent. Rather than always saying yes, we now say no. Whatever the case, instead of repressing feelings or fostering destructive behavior, our challenge is to accept and listen to what our anger is expressing. Then, we can think of constructive and healing ways to cope with anger as well as its underlying feelings. Middle-age desert solitude lends itself to such discovery.

Some middle-agers feel that life has gone "down the drain," and they blame others for mistreating them. Indeed, their anger and resentment often indicate an uncomfortable truth: many middle-agers have been mistreated. Abused middle-agers can be aware of what has happened and, without being vindictive, take responsibility for changing their lives.

As always, there are many human, but deleterious, ways of dealing with desert emergence. A recurrent obstacle at any age is to "double feel," that is, to feel negatively about a feeling. For instance, we can feel depressed about being depressed or angry about being angry. Though common, such coping is not healthy and it exacerbates the pain and tension. Alcohol and other drugs as well as obsessive-compulsive behavior also impede healthy self-emergence.

Another obstacle is that, too often, well-intentioned persons try to help middle-agers in negative ways; they sincerely offer help that hinders. Family, friends, and professionals may pressure us to be our "old selves," provoking us to feel guilty for what we experience. Such help assumes that feelings of depression and anger are necessarily unhealthy and should be purged rather than respected. It behooves middle-agers to be aware of sincere, yet negative, help.

Psychological and social stress is normal in middle age. For instance, it is the time of the "empty nest." Women or men who have focused their lives on their children are thrown into a crisis when the children leave. No longer can they invest their time, energy, and love in their children. Now they feel lost. Actually, they have good reason to feel depressed about such a state of affairs; nevertheless, their challenge is to renew themselves. The desert is an opportunity to do just that.

A common way to escape the pain of self-awareness is to turn to alcohol. Alcoholism, a major problem for men between the ages of forty-five and sixty-four, can be an attempt to numb feelings of depression, loneliness, and personal failure. Most important, these spirits can numb the Spirit.

A successful resolution to middle-age issues leads to an easier resolution in the elder years. Women often adjust better than men to the elder years partly because women work through their middle-age passage better than men. They learn to be more independent, stronger, and endure more than men as they grow older. Adjusting to environmental changes and facing the pain of self-renewal, women build a strong foundation for the second half of their adult lives.

Fundamental questions about sexuality are asked. Am I still a man? Am I still a woman? Have I been an authentic male or female person? Will I continue to be one? Too many men and women feel insecure about their primary sexuality and, consequently, doubt themselves. If we have focused too much on physical attraction and functional performance, we can undergo a painful crisis. Men who emphasize genital sex at the expense of other expressions of sexuality can be in dire difficulty. For others, however, middle age is an excellent time to deepen the efforts already started in midlife—to become a more integral sexual person.

Genital sex comes to a clear crisis. Researchers indicate that people who have withdrawn from genital sex find it increasingly difficult to reenter it. Studies show that male sexual inadequacy increases sharply after age fifty. The prognosis is poor for those who assume that they are "too old" for such things and who have not consistently practiced loving sex.

In the lonely trails of the middle-age desert, we can feel lost, unloved, and unworthy of love. Even though loved ones tell us that they love us, we can feel deserted and we doubt them. Though we cognitively know that others love us, we feel alone and uncomfortably empty. Too often, friends and family, with good intentions, encourage us to be our old selves instead of inviting us to renew ourselves. Some embrace us no matter what, including our doubts and changes in behavior.

Once again, spirituality is paramount in managing these changes as well as improving the quality of our lives. A spiritual challenge is to connect with transcendent love that helps us to accept and cope with our changes. We experience the healing community that is there with us and goes infinitely beyond our problems. Bonding with God enables us to be more compassionate toward ourselves and others as well as to cope more effectively.

Especially in the absence of interpersonal intimacy, we hunger for the intimacy that always nourishes. Starving for more than what we alone can give ourselves, we admit our radical poverty—that we cannot save ourselves. Always being in, with, and through God enables us to think, decide, and act effectively. Divine connection empowers us. Even more important, we comfort, console, and care more effectively as well as being more comforted, consoled, and cared for. We experience the healing power of Uncreated Love.

We again affirm and deepen our radical dependency on the Source of our powers. We reaffirm that we alone are powerless in making permanent sense of our human condition and that, on our own, we can ultimately do little. We surrender to a power of Love that is greater than and yet embraces us. We give up trying to control our destiny and accept and follow our call. Rather than futilely trying to save ourselves, we surrender to God. Then our emptiness is fulfilled; our helplessness engenders power; our poverty begets riches; our darkness elicits light; and our loneliness evokes love.

If we have derived too much of our worth from work, we are likely to undergo a painful reevaluation. Feeling physically tired, psychologically drained, and socially disenchanted, we can experience a spiritual crisis of work. Work calls for significance. If our paid work cannot become a way to improve life, we may become involved in community and religious activities. We want some of our work to count.

Paradoxically, our relative lack of vitality can lead to new vitality. We are challenged to recreate so that play with ourselves and others is renewed. Play is especially useful in fostering a gentle and spirited mode of being as well as a common ground for being with others. Having more time and different energy, we manifest more consistently a playful spirit wherever we are. In playing with Spirit, we celebrate everyday living.

In growing older, death and dying become clearly critical. If we have run from death, it usually catches us at this time. Though some of us can still escape the grasp of death, we will eventually be caught in our elder years. The tragedy of escaping death is that we consequently miss much of life. Middle age offers us a special opportunity to accept death and, therefore, increase life.

If we have denied death most of our lives, the grand inquisitor now demands to be heard. No longer does death whisper, silently open our door, or walk into our room; death comes up to us, shakes hands, and speaks loudly and clearly. Death looks at us, touches us, and talks to us. Death holds us and asks us how and why we have been living. Death pleads with us to live. Our dreadful response can be our saving grace.

Death of loved ones, which is likely to occur at this time, radically changes our lives. When a beloved one dies, our present experience, past memories, and future possibilities change significantly. Such a death creates experiential gaps in personal and community relationships. Hopefully, death helps us appreciate the value of life and encourages us to live virtuously. We know how death becomes a life force that motivates integral and spiritual living. Such a deeper awareness and appreciation of death enables us to enjoy life more than ever, perhaps to transcend death by touching eternal life. Rather than living a depressed life waiting to die, the desert of middle age is the way to a more spirited and joyful life.

Every transition to a new decade is a milestone. Our sixtieth birthday drops us on the threshold of the elder years. For more than a few people, it is more difficult than becoming fifty. For others, being sixty promises more freedom from work and freedom for a new lifestyle. Whatever the experience, the big six-zero makes us late middle-agers who are soon to enter the generation of the young elderly.

Changes continue to occur. Friends, peers, and especially parents are nearing death or have died. We go to the weddings of our children and of the children of relatives and friends. Since we feel older and are becoming the senior family members, we take more responsibility in family and community affairs. We become the leaders. We take the place of our parents. Soon we will be members of the "alpha" generation—the oldest and last generation.

Actually, parent-child roles may reverse somewhat. Sometimes, especially if we have not had much contact with our parents, we may know them for the first time outside their parental roles. This can cause difficulties or present opportunities for both parents and middle-aged children. Old, repressed problems may emerge and cause hurt and resentment. On the other hand, we and our parents can become companions and learn to enjoy each other more than ever.

Age evokes memories. A married couple may look at their married daughters and sons and feel that it was only yesterday that they were children. They may even see themselves as grandparents more than as parents. Where has the time gone? And yet, we might not feel as old as we are. We still feel young in our aging bodies. Middle-age milestones incorporate a history that makes for fulfillment or emptiness.

Middle age welcomes reconciliation and calls us to community with ourselves, others, and God. We have seen that our way to healing and oneness is paradoxical. Depression pressures us to achieve a sense of fulfillment. Guilt beckons us to forgive ourselves and others. Limits move us to the Unlimited. Loneliness prepares us for Love. Resentment teaches us to be compassionate and forgiving. Nothingness proclaims Being. This is the age of atonement—to become one with ourselves and others. The time is for joy.

LAND OF JOY

Middle age can be a joyful time to harvest the fruits of desert planting, or it can be a barren land with little hope. Since middle age can last fifteen or more years, it offers a long time of misery or joy.

Middle age is our last time of being "not old." Although these years are times of settling down rather than restructuring life, the fifties include preparing for the elder years. Future economic security becomes increasingly important, and for good reason, because it increases the likelihood of physical and psychological safety and comfort as well as opening up opportunities for learning and leisure. Living a spiritual life is of paramount importance. All activities diminish in meaning without a spiritual life.

During these years of becoming older, it is wise to keep ourselves in good physical, psychosocial, and spiritual condition. To keep our activity level consistent, rather than sporadic, and to maintain a nutritious, low-calorie diet can be important. Although we may not eat as much, we can enjoy each meal as a small feast. Sleeping habits may change, but we can enjoy sleep and view it as a way to recuperate. Activity is then valued more by its quality than by its quantity. In this way, we come to a new physical vigor. Resisting the temptation to succumb to ageism—to become tired, flabby, and sedentary—we take physical care and exercise. We become adept at self-expression that manifests a gentle and graceful touch. We can truly become an embodiment of Spirit.

To slow down and to see life in its sacred dimensions can bring a wealth of fulfillment. Such active slowing down can bring on inner activity that evokes more quiet enthusiasm than external hyperactivity. Most middle-agers have more opportunity to slow down, to enjoy, to take vacations, to see things differently, and to do nothing. For instance, to experience spirituality in everyday living as well as to observe special occasions such as feast days and holy days, adds significantly to the quality of our lives.

Wisdom becomes a central motivating force. Though wisdom is not absent before middle age, it now blossoms. Seeing through the eyes of eternity, we see light in darkness and darkness in light. Seeing with our inner eye, we appreciate more than our senses allow. Knowing by unknowing, we understand more than is rationally possible. When life darkens and seems impossible, we see light and possibilities. We know that there is a time for all seasons. We smile with compassion.

Practical wisdoms give us a good measure of common sense so that our judgments are prudent rather than compulsive or impulsive.

We are unlikely to be lured down blind alleys and more likely to cope well. By this time, most of us have learned some strategies that help to lessen the wear and tear of normal living. We have learned how to reduce the internal and external sources of debilitating stress as well as fostering healthy experiences.

We usually find new interests or new old ones. We take time to enjoy activities, arts, reading, and people. Becoming grandparents may enable us to renew playful times or compensate for missed opportunities with our own children. If celibate, we become grandpersons who can touch in wisdom and love. Knowing now, from experience, what pleases and fulfills, we might take courses or join groups that promote self-improvement and social concern.

Besides becoming members of an economically powerful generation, we can come closer to communion with one another. Above all, we deepen our community ties by celebrating its binding force—the Spirit of God. Rather than growing in resentment and bitterness over past injustices and failures as well as missed opportunities, we can enjoy communal living. For example, married people now have more time to be with each other socially, sexually, and spiritually. Their spousal union of head and heart, their sharing and fostering of mutual values, and their spiritual oneness increase. While respecting each other's need for solitude and individuality, they come closer to being one.

Vowed celibates can also deepen their communal lives. They more fully realize that celibacy offers more opportunities (than married life) to be alone with God. Not being committed to a spouse liberates them to be more available for others. Paradoxically, their celibacy (being alone) fosters community.

Middle age can also be the time to reap the fruits of our interpersonal labor. We can take delight in knowing that we have influenced others in becoming responsible adults. We can begin to see how our interpersonal struggles and sacrifices have led to better relationships. We can experience joy and satisfaction in being veteran members of a community.

As middle-agers, we are more aware of ourselves and one another, and we can communicate in a way that fosters communion. Men can be more gentle and affectionate, and women can freely proclaim themselves. Furthermore, fewer gender differences are apparent in activities, interests, and interpersonal relationships. As men and women, we come closer to being one of a kind.

Spiritual meaning can now be experienced, more than ever, in everyone and in everything. Seeing with spiritual eyes enables us to enjoy an inexhaustible source of fulfilling meaning. Paradoxically, we experience *more* than we experience. We realize that there is more to life than what happens to us. We live with a perpetual sense of surprise, with a sense that each day, each hour, and each moment, something full of wonder may happen. The ordinary becomes extraordinary. Kairotic times become more frequent and evident.

Such contemplative living is active. It is not magical musing, sentimental self-deception, or spiritualistic nonsense. It is concrete, practical, and fulfilling. It is a different way of seeing and being; it is a way that transcends and enriches everyday living.

We also see spirituality where it is hidden. We know that people who are living mad or bad lives are actually unhappy, for they miss life's Source of power and care. We appeal to the Spirit in them. Rather than trying to convince them of the Spirit, we respond to their spirit in their apparent nonsense. This contemplative view pierces through the armor of evil and madness to underlying goodness.

Transcendent love nears fruition in middle age. Unconditional love becomes less of a theoretical fantasy and more of an experiential reality. Transcendent love means that we relate without needing anything from anyone. No longer do we need another to respond in kind; no longer do we need another to love, respect, listen to, or understand us; and no longer do we need another to stop being unfair, cruel, evil, or sick. At first, this orientation of needing nothing from anyone may sound isolating, indifferent, detached without love, callous, or sick. On the contrary, such a way of being promotes healthier intimacy, is more caring and involved, and is more healing and hopeful. Why and how is this so?

We have seen that, when we need love from a particular person, we put our well-being in that person's hands. Consequences of this needy love include empowering and burdening the other as well as avoiding taking responsibility for our own welfare. Such a posture—to need love from another person—is appropriate for a child who is necessarily dependent on caretakers, but it is inappropriate for adults.

In middle age, this ideal of pure giving comes of age. We realize that we do need love (respect, consolation, guidance, understanding, etc.), but not from any particular person, except God. Thus, although we do not need a "particular person" (friend, parent, child, sibling, spouse) to love us, we do need to love and be loved by "people."

So, transcendent love means that we connect with God and others in love via friends, support groups, religion, solitude, prayer, animals, plants, and life. Persons whom we love and who love us are interjected and incorporated within us. Within ourselves dwells a community that is there for us in love. Thus, we are never alone.

Acting out of "we" rather than "me" enables us to accept not receiving what we "want" but do not "need." For example, I do not need you to love me because I give and receive love from my community—God, self, and others—that dwells within me. Indeed, I want you to love me, for life is better and easier for both of us when we love each other. When you are mean, narcissistic, manipulative, or indifferent to me, I still hurt, but significantly less when I am bonded with my inner community. In, through, and with God and others, I can give without needing you to give to me.

Such a spiritual approach combats unhealthy relationships such as codependent, dependent, aggressive, and avoidant ones, and increases the likelihood of healthier relationships. Being free, serene, and strong makes a powerful impact on others. Even in the midst of turmoil where there is no external peace, we can be serene. Like reeds in a turbulent storm, we can remain rooted. And, like redwoods in the silent forest, we stand solid and tall.

Sometimes, and unfortunately, "detached love" is appropriate. So-called detached love is difficult to practice, for it can be a demanding measure of true love. Most important, detached love is unconditional and there is no expectation of our needs being satisfied. We abstain from fixing or making others be or behave the way we want or need. We refuse to take their behavior personally and to take offense. Although we disagree or even hate their behavior, we try to accept and love them.

Not only do we let people make choices, but we also let them take the consequences of their behavior. This is not easy, particularly with someone you love. We realize that to interfere or take responsibility for them usually impedes growth. Because of love, we refuse to enable their negative behavior and remain present, yet detached. Rather than using arguments, threats, pleasing, caretaking, or avoidance to get them to see our light, we step out of their way so that the Light may shine on them.

Such detached love is especially needed with addicts, coaddicts, mentally ill persons, and bad people. To be sure, setting boundaries that prevent harm to self and others is part of such difficult love. To intervene when there is serious harm to self or others is needed. Always, to let go of manipulation and to let God help us is the paramount way to heal and reconcile.

Compassion broadens and deepens. In compassion, we help one another bear the weight of our problems, our pain, and our lives. Rather than becoming alienated from others and falling into isolated loneliness, we strive to respond in love to everyone. We are sometimes comfortably attached and sometimes carefully detached. Love can be easy and love can be tough. Being dependent only on God as our perpetual source of love enables us to give, without expectation of return, in the best and worst of times.

We have seen that middle age is a prime time to mature, when transcendence is deepened qualitatively and quantitatively. When we experience the Source of Life, our lives are meaningful no matter what. We really celebrate everyday living and praise God's Being in all beings. Instead of settling for much less than is possible, instead of focusing on reality's surface, and instead of living nervously and restlessly without purpose and direction, we transcend to a deep and sustaining source of consolation and enlightenment.

In the midst of aging, healthy middle-agers foster a playful and loving style of living—a life of celebration. Celebrations structure chronological times for engendering and remembering kairotic events. They enable us to enjoy the reason for and ground of our beings. To stand in awe, to give thanks and praise, to laugh and cry, and to eat and drink with Spirit rekindles and affirms the sacred times while renewing our spirits. With Spirit, we dance.

Chapter 10

The Elder Years

A popular assumption in Western culture is that the elder years mark the end, rather than the zenith, of life. Looking toward old age with controlled trepidation rather than joyful expectation, we fail to appreciate these last years of adulthood. Our aim is to present the elder years as the most spirited time on earth, when the spirit of life is most fully and integrally manifested. Indeed, this season can be a time of feasting, not of famine. It can be a time for a spiritual banquet.

Perhaps because of our fears of old age, much money and effort have been invested in the study of being elderly (gerontology) and the treatment of elderly people (geriatrics). Studies on aging, genetic inheritance, economic stability, nutrition, and medical care have increased. Educational, political, social, and recreational organizations and programs for the elderly have also multiplied. The area that has been neglected, however, is spirituality. This is unfortunate for any age group, but especially so for those who are peaking spiritually. Thus, our focus, even more than with the previous stages of development, is on the spiritual life.

A familiar sight emerges on the horizon of the elder years—the desert. Rather than being surprised by such a vision, seasoned travelers welcome it and make the journey, perhaps for the last time. Standing on its threshold, we are less inclined to regress to slavery and more likely to accept its invitation to enter its dark splendor. Hopefully, we know by now that the desert heals, strengthens, and enlightens.

DESERT OF DEATH

Every desert is a crisis of life and death—and at no other time is death so insistent as in the elder years. How do we respond to the critical questions of impending death? Do we respond to death with life? Or are we still futilely trying to escape death? Do we disengage not only from social activities but also from life itself, or do we engage life more deeply? Is our spirit manifested more strongly and clearly, or is our spirit dying? Can we say yes to our past and affirm our future? Or do we seek to escape from life, rationalize its meaning, and deny its value? The bottom line is that eternal life is the only adequate answer to death's questions.

No longer are we thinking about death; no longer is death peeking through the keyhole; no longer does death talk to us; and no longer does death shake hands. Now, death embraces us. Is death a friend or an enemy? Have we faced death as a friend, or have we run from death as from an enemy? Have we tried to deny the obvious? Can we continue to say yes to an unknown future that incorporates an inescapable death? Can we face death? Can we look at death's stare with eyes of eternal life? Can we conquer death with life?

If we have listened to death in our middle age and before, it will hold little terror for us now. The desert of death, however, can look overwhelming if we have denied death. Then, rather than reaching its zenith, life becomes meaningless and inert. Instead of leading to despair, this final desert can be our saving grace. It can be experienced as a springboard to eternal life.

Embracing death is a redemptive force. When death embraces us, we return the embrace. We accept that we are powerless over death, and we surrender our life and will to God (or a Higher Power) who gives us life. Such acceptance and communion evoke an enormous sense of power and vision that no one can take from us. When we accept death, nothing else can harm us. In dying, we destroy death and restore life.

Our final milestone is death. For the last time, death beckons us to live. To say yes to life means that life has been meaningful. If life has been an escape from death, then death can be devastating and absolute. Death is the end; there is no new life.

We realize that not only are we going to die, but we are also dying. Soon after the moment of conception, we begin to die in order to live. If we remained as one cell, not much life would evolve. Likewise, if we fixate in childhood, adolescence, young adulthood, or any time, we fail to live as well as we can. We must die to where we are in order to grow. Yet paradoxically, when we die to a time of life, we live even more. Like the acorn that must die to become an oak, while remaining part of the tree, we must die in order to become more of ourselves while remaining ourselves. Thus, through the process of living and dying, we change and remain the same.

It is good to remember that we are always on our deathbeds. Thinking of ourselves in our last moments can bring life into perspective. In spite of our limitations and sins, can we say that we are living a life of love? Despite all imperfections, defects, and vices, can we say that we have tried to do the best we can? Can we say that we have journeyed through the deserts as well as through the promised lands? Though we may have been tempted to escape and may even have escaped temporarily, have we always come back to weather the storms? Can we say that we have never intentionally manipulated or exploited people? Can we say that we have never purposely violated life? If we did, can we say that we have repented and have been reconciled? Even though we may have been crippled, have we continued to dance with life?

Persons who have grown with death find it relatively easy to face death. Death is no stranger. Still, it is not entirely comfortable, for death is a powerful force that throws us back to our beginnings. It is an unknown and uncontrollable reality that cuts through all of life. Thus, to be afraid of death is normal, but to have the courage to face the dread of death evokes life.

If we have escaped from the desert of death, we will have difficult times coming to the promised land of joy. And yet, the final desert calls us one last time for the journey to the promised land. A denial of death, a repression of painful feelings such as depression and loneliness, and the identification of life with function are key attitudinal obstacles.

However, death can be ugly. Although we know we are dying and will die, we do not know the time, place, or manner of our last times. Deaths vary: some people pass over peacefully, while others suffer a living hell. The hospice way of dying can be invaluable in transforming an ugly death to a beautiful farewell. Hospice caretakers minister to the dying with life.

We can be hospitable with death. As we did with the beginning of a new life, we can be good hosts. First, we prepare for death the same way that we prepared for birth. We make room for dying persons. We invite them into our hearts so that they are not alone. We are attentive to their needs, making them as comfortable as possible and listening and seeing with deep reverence and respect. We show our love for them at conception, at birth, during the life cycle, at death, and thereafter. From the beginning to the end, we are present in love.

Death persistently asks how and why we are living, while life awaits our answers. It raises questions about integrity. Am I whole? Am I a truthful person in touch with my whole self and with others? Have I merely lived a cerebral existence? Have I placed too much emphasis on what I have, rather than who I am? Those who have lived a fragmented and disassociated life feel displaced, anxiously groundless, and out of touch with the heart of the matter.

Along with integrity, we question our worth. Where does my worth lie? What is my worth? Am I worthwhile? Do I appreciate my own dignity? Has life been worth the struggle? Am I worthy of love and of life? Do I feel worthless? An absolute nothing? Do I mean something to someone? To myself? To God? Will I be missed when I die? Will I be remembered by those who love me?

Our need for God increases as we grow older. We realize that we cannot save ourselves. Our redemption lies in becoming companions with the Person who is the Sustaining Source of our dignity, integrity, and being. We can sit down with our Creator, converse, give thanks, break bread, and be healed. The desert of isolation is conquered with life. No matter what illness, deprivation, loneliness, or rejection, we humbly appreciate the truth that we are people of infinite worth and that we are never alone.

A life rooted in God's love manifests dignity and seeks meaning and fulfillment in all circumstances. However, if we have displaced God's love, even though we may be surrounded by everything we ever wanted, we come to nothingness. Our past charades become senseless and no longer evoke applause. Life becomes radically frustrating and ultimately terminal.

There is always hope. Even if we have escaped the desert, the crisis of the elder years can be an invitation to discover our lost spirit. Even though we see little sense to life, we still have time to say yes to the present and the future, and ask to be forgiven for the past. In reconciling ourselves, we realize that our integrity and dignity are grounded in God who is the uncreated and perpetual Source of all virtues. Rather than finding life empty, we can come closer to being permanently fulfilled in the kingdom of God.

We are challenged in a new way to love and suffer. Do we alienate ourselves from others and become bitter and fester in resentment? Do we see everyone as "out there" rather than being part of us? Can we understand and cope with the cultural madness of ageism, while forgiving it? Can we offer our suffering as a sacrifice—an act that makes life sacred and redemptive? Can we suffer in service of individual and communal growth? Can love (from God, ourselves, and others) heal our pain and liberate us to care unconditionally?

Being called to reflect on our commitment to love never ends. With the years running short, we can deepen our marital commitment. If widowed, it becomes important to adjust to loneliness as well as to economic, medical, and social problems. If single, our reference groups can provide occasions for sharing values and interests as well as giving understanding and support. We are members of a community, we continue to care and let others care for us. If we have lived without love, we can be terrified by our impending death, or the crisis can prod us to find a permanent sense of everlasting life.

In spite of physiological decline, we can embody our spirits more powerfully than ever. Centering ourselves in the Spirit, we can critique the cultural trend to overemphasize the physical and functional. For instance, our arthritic hands can show more spirit and beauty than our once-sensual young hands. We can better touch and be touched. We can also understand and respond to the embodiment of others. Incarnating the Spirit, we are infinitely present and touchable.

Some elderly people disengage from social activities. Although various senior citizens' groups offer healthy activities, many elderly, especially men, are still inclined to be uninvolved. Although our economic status influences our activities and interests to some degree, there is no need for us, rich or poor, to become socially dead. In fact, our spiritual crisis can engender a new social interest. Becoming more spiritual, we can derive even more joy from vacations, trips, walks, reading, media, and, especially, celebrating the routine of living.

The inevitable fact is that the elder years call forth spirituality more than before. We are, more than ever, able to transcend, that is, to go beyond our physical, social, and psychological confinement. The desert of death reaffirms and helps us to experience the unity that underlies all of our differences. We experience all races, sexes, ethnic groups, and ages as parts of the same reality. Still, we can be seduced by the false belief that we are primarily individuals, rather than interwoven members of the same community. Our saving grace is to respond to the proclamation of the "more than"—that all people and all things are interconnected. We appreciate that all of us are varied manifestations of the same Uncreated Love.

But some of us withdraw and grow grumpy, and people may wonder what is happening to us. A common reason for our testy behavior may be that we have identified life with work and minimized life's nonfunctional, spiritual dimensions. We have learned to value usefulness, control, information, and something rather than uselessness, being, surrender, formation, and nothing. Rather than being recognized as we once were, now we may be tolerated, criticized, or misunderstood because it is assumed that we serve no valuable purpose.

Consider retirement. Too many of us leave the last day of work on Friday, enjoy Saturday and Sunday, and get up for work on Monday. Finding that we have no work, we relax. But, on Monday afternoon, we begin to seek things to do. After a few days, when we have fixed everything twice, we search for anything to do. In due course, after forcing ourselves to be active, we have to come back to ourselves. We have to realize that identifying life with work is not the best way. We can learn and enjoy the art of doing nothing.

Another difficulty that we must face is the significant difference that often lies between the expectations and the realities of retirement. For example, we may expect to live more fully in retirement, but socioeconomic problems impede the achievement of our goals. Some of us never prepare for retirement and falsely assume that things will work out.

Women usually adjust better than men to the relative absence of work because, unlike most men, women maintain many of their domestic and interpersonal activities. As we grow older, the personal and interpersonal become more consistent and real. Men should observe and learn from women the art of being and being with. It is often advisable to find part-time work as a consultant or a volunteer. Such activity brings meaning and bridges the gap between middle and elder years.

Unfortunately, the elderly often find themselves by themselves. The death of a spouse is likely to cause a difficult adjustment to living with and by oneself. A man, for instance, who has been dependent on his wife in domestic and personal matters can feel depressed, lost, and helpless without her. Although women are more likely to find themselves alone because they are likely to marry at a younger age and live more than seven years longer than men, women still tend to adjust to being alone better than men. They are usually more socially adept and better at taking care of themselves.

Some couples are fortunate to live together well into their elder years. If they have lived authentically with each other, these years are their happiest. They have grown and continue to grow older together in love. However, couples who have gone their separate ways will probably be miserable. Their efforts to adjust to their situation often lead to withdrawal from each other, leaving them alone and lonely. They become strangers living together.

Furthermore, the elderly often lose the authority they once had in the family and in society. Instead of giving them genuine respect, we often patronize and tolerate them. We seldom go to them for advice and comfort. This is ironic because the elderly can be the most qualified to console and sustain us, especially spiritually. When we minimize spirituality, we have less reason to consult them. Indeed, some elderly people are far from being spiritual counselors and, instead, are irritable and authoritarian. Nevertheless, even they are less likely to play interpersonal games and more likely to speak the truth.

Whatever the reason, loneliness is common in the desert. It is difficult to love someone who is absent. The challenge is to discover transcendent love, to love people, life, ourselves, and God in both their absence and presence. As we discovered in midlife, we do not depend totally or even primarily on people, but on God as our consoling Source of Life.

Most important is to love and be loved by God. God's love is always our saving grace, especially when no humans directly love us. Our ultimate dependence on God culminates in the elder years. No matter what our physical, social, and psychological conditions may be, God offers us life. Growing older in love enables us to depend on and enjoy the Spirit of Life. With God, we are never alone and always alive, for God is the beginning and the perpetual end of Life. In short, God is Uncreated Life that/who gives us everlasting life.

Those of us who have not known love may be horrified. Loneliness has caught us. If we have only learned to adjust to each other, but failed to grow in community, we will feel lost and empty in the absence of love. No further escape is possible. The demand of life that we live in love screams out at us. It is our final hope—our final summons to live a life of love—to journey to the promised land.

Many factors influence our final journey. For example, those of us who assume that old age is diminution rather than culmination of life can be devastated in our elder years. Persons who are part of a supportive family, religious community, or who have close friends are likely to fare better than those who are single or widowed. Isolation engenders and exacerbates lifelessness. Although happiness is not primarily a result of money, financial resources are necessary to satisfy basic needs and to open up certain opportunities. Few persons enjoy aesthetic and spiritual living if their basic needs are not met.

It is imperative in the elder years to rekindle, to reaffirm, and to nourish our spiritual lives. Because we have more time to listen to the Spirit, we run the risk of postponing our spiritual concerns. While changes in personal and social situations demand adjustments, spiritual needs are less pressing and rarely encouraged. We have to be careful that we do not adjust psychosocially and forget spiritual growth.

Becoming relatively disengaged from previous roles and functional responsibilities can help us to deepen our spiritual lives. Rather than finding activities that simply fill up time, we can look for activities that rekindle and renew the spirit. Such an approach is not difficult to follow if it has been cultivated for years before retirement. Since we are less easily seduced by the cultural madness about us, we are freer to hear and respond to the Spirit of Life in ourselves and others. Being somewhat detached from conventional life enables us to see abnormally, that is, to see more than is normally seen.

Our past lives offer major obstacles or aids to living through the elder years. Those of us who have forgotten, repressed, or displaced God have difficulty becoming old and happy. Facing death without God is tragic. Our crisis will probably fracture our madness and call attention to what we have missed. In authentic living, normal madness makes little sense in the elder years mainly because it seldom pays dividends.

Another obstacle to growth is the prejudice against being old—ageism. This cultural force can engender loneliness as well as feelings of worthlessness. A youth-oriented culture that judges people on their usefulness and sees little of the elderly's transcendent value. Our culture seldom learns from the elderly, but rather sees them as a problem to be dealt with, a people who need to be treated and controlled. Without spirituality, the elderly can easily be seen as worthless and burdensome, and we lose our most valuable resource. Worst of all, the elderly can see themselves in these ageist ways.

To transcend this cultural barbarism, a spiritual approach is very helpful. Spirituality leads to an acceptance and compassion for all people, even those who violate or forget the elderly. The spiritual life enables us to say "yes" no matter what and to see meaning in the midst of oppression.

Our final dark night enlightens us and fills us with hope. This is our last Lent before we come to our eternal Easter. If we have run from life till now, this final Lent can be a saving grace that leads to resurrection. We must be patient. We must be willing to wait and suffer in love, and to stay in the desert, rather than seek to escape it. Otherwise, we may die without being redeemed. We must believe that life presents us with fasts, Advents, and Lents that promise feasts, Christmases, and Easters.

LAND OF LIFE

After the desert of old age, which may be either a devastating or a relatively easy journey, we settle down for the last time. Whether or not these short or long years are meaningful is certainly influenced by social, economic, medical, and other environmental factors, but the paramount factor is spirituality. Even in the midst of poverty and oppression, life can be good and dignified when based on spirituality. Experiencing the Infinite within us, our dignity touches people.

However, our connection with the Infinite may intimidate some people. Reactively, they minimize or dismiss our value rather than accepting and benefiting from it. Such an approach is especially evident in mass media. For example, television seldom shows spirituality in a preferred light, but is more likely to celebrate situations without spirit.

We can break through the false myth that old age is meaningless and horrible. In spite of ageism, disease, or economic oppression, we can be happier than anyone else. Rather than succumbing to a premature death or identifying life with physical activity or functional success, we can spiritually dance and laugh with life. We see through the madness of ageism, while being compassionate and forgiving with its proponents.

The elder years bring the milestones of retirement, being together with spouse or community in a new way, and children who make us "grand" parents, uncles, and friends. Being members of the oldest or "alpha" generation brings new limits and possibilities, new oppression and opportunity. More than ever, we are moved to place less emphasis on the functional and to be open to new visions, new thoughts, new decisions, new behaviors, and new life.

Looking back on life, we can say that we have run the good race and that we have given our best. Rather than empty desolation, life is fulfilling and consoling. Even though we are surrounded by the absence of loved ones, we feel present to them in their absence. Out there beyond our reach, we still touch and are touched. Indeed, we transcend our limits and go beyond the surface by constantly experiencing the Unlimited and Inexhaustible Ground of our being. Wherever and whenever we look, we experience the Spirit of Life. We experience being connected to and part of more than our individual selves.

The elder years bring an appreciation of how easy it is to be seduced by the counterfeits of the Spirit. We understand that pleasure and success are only temporary fulfillments that fail to last. We see that the mania for having material possessions offers sparse profit compared to the measure of being. Even though our search for the Spirit was frequently detoured, the Spirit never left us. The Source of Life, our Holy Spirit, was and is always with us. We now have a pure vision of the soul of life, and being in the consoling presence of the Holy Spirit enables us to rest in peace.

In old age, we can look back with a compassionate smile at our attempts to be absolutely fulfilled. We know now that absolute satisfaction and enjoyment are never possible and ultimately inconsequential. Life always did and always will incorporate unfulfillment, discontent, unhappiness, misery, and pain along with fulfillment, contentment, happiness, joy, and pleasure. We let go of false promises of self-fulfillment, self-actualization, self-esteem, self-assertion, self-satisfaction, self-determination, of *self,* and bear with joy the process of becoming older together in Love.

Earth is a journey to heaven. Although moments of heaven are experienced on earth, absolute fulfillment only comes after we finally stop dying and finally live forever. Nevertheless, in the elder years we can feel more serenity, closer to eternal life, and nearer to the kingdom of God. Rather than feeling wiped out, we feel we are returning home. Realizing that life has been a search for home, we look back with gratitude and hope for the future, and feel consoled in the present.

Love permeates life. Although there may be few people near or with us, we are in Love. Despite environmental deprivation, serenity resides in the core of our being when we rest in Love. When we live in Love, nothing much is foreign, for all life is familiar. Rather than being restless, jumpy, and lost, we feel that soon we will be home to rest eternally in Love. However, those of us who have run from the desert will have a difficult time believing in God's promised land of love. Love's substitutes of success, pleasure, power, social recognition, and psychological adjustment only end in desolation. So, we are left with nothing, which could lead to our saving grace.

More than any other time, the elder years call for transcendent autonomy. An impediment to such freedom is to play the game of being old: being passive, dependent, dumb, and burdensome rather than claiming our lives in the Infinite. Authentic autonomy is rooted in our spiritual lives. Our laws for living are informed and formed by transcendent rather than only rational realities. In this way, it is possible to reach the zenith of autonomy even though we are dependent physically and socially. We can be free in a concentration camp, in a warehouse for old people, or in a rejecting family or community. By God, we are free.

In spite of physical, social, and economic dependence, we can be truly independent when we freely depend on God. If we have grown throughout life in freedom's Spirit, our elder years culminate in freedom. Paradoxically, the highest form of autonomy is rooted in and sustained by dependence when we affirm our original and perpetual reliance on God.

Some of us become more active than ever before. We may join senior citizens' clubs that offer opportunities for recreation and travel at relatively low cost. Furthermore, we can enjoy everyday living such as eating, sleeping, walking, and talking. For example, the elderly often relive their lives in dreams so that sleep becomes an enjoyable experience. The elder years also offer more opportunities to do nothing rather than something, to enjoy the useless rather than the useful, and to live in community rather than simply managing to cope. But if we have run from life, our dreams may become nightmares and past, pleasurable escapes prove to be futile. Overdrinking and overeating are practically fatal. The elder years call for authentic play—a play filled with Spirit.

Our journey is nearing its end. The process of dying will soon cease; living will soon be permanent. We feel permanence is on its way, that nothing temporary lasts, and that all temporary things call for the permanent. Seeing the permanent emerging on the horizon and coming closer gives a vision that we never had so clearly before, a vision that helps us accept life and claim the future.

Without spirituality, life becomes at best gloomy and at worst meaningless. If primary meaning comes from being in good physical health, achieving functional success, or feeling contented, then life eventually becomes absurd. Such a life becomes a constant escape from death, resurrection, and reconciliation. Especially in old age, when physical and social maladies are more pervasive, life dissipates without a spiritual vision. Without Spirit, there is no life.

Those who have escaped the challenge to grow throughout life are more likely to suffer mental illness or attempt suicide in the elder years. Those who enter their seventies only to discover that life has been a charade can easily despair. In fact, suicide reaches its maximum rate for males between the ages of seventy-five and eighty-four. If we are accustomed to using money and power as escapes from spiritual questions, we end up with nothing. Finally, we have to face the radical issues of life and death.

Some of us see the elderly as worn-out, nonproductive, accident-prone, worthless, and hard to live and be with. Others take a more positive view of the elderly as valuable and worthy of being with. How we see them determines to a high degree how we treat them. Although we may talk about the elderly in positive terms, we must honestly ask ourselves how we concretely behave toward them. Do we simply tolerate them, or do we care for and learn from them? Can we—young and old—sing and dance together?

We usually feel uncomfortable when we think of sexuality in the elder years. We make pathetic jokes about it or simply ignore it. The fact is that elderly people can have an enjoyable sex life. When we practice sexuality as an art of intimacy and integrate it with spirituality, it becomes satisfying and fulfilling. The quantity of genital relations invariably decreases as compared with younger years, but its quality can increase. We can have more sexual know-how—primarily from knowing each other better and being less likely to be sexist and ageist. We can enjoy the Spirit of sex.

We continue to be more androgynous. Growing older together means becoming more alike, though never the same. Affectively, we can reach out, touch, and communicate in innumerable ways. Actually, our sexuality leads more and more to a contemplative vision and appreciation of one another. Now a glance can convey a message of a lifetime and a promise of a future.

Our past attitudes and practices highly determine our sexual lives in later years. If we integrate love and sexuality, we remain active and share a fulfilling relationship. However, a fragmented sexual life contributes nothing to the elder years. A "macho" man who has identified sexuality with genitality will probably be impotent and have no interest in incorporating female qualities into his life. A woman who has accepted the cultural expectation of becoming neuter in middle age will probably find herself "neuterized" in old age.

Love in the elder years often takes on a fidelity that includes the asceticism to accept pain. For example, to suffer from physical ailments as well as social oppression, personal rejection, and general injustice can be a clear and constant form of suffering love. Such love is accepted without complaint or the need to have the pain taken away. We realize that pain is necessary for reconciling growth and that death will finally lead to painless living. Such redemptive love is based on our primary commitment to God and others who give us the courage and strength to love unconditionally.

A common danger is isolation—for the elderly to alienate themselves or to be avoided by others, or both, which only compounds their pain, confusion, and isolation. An essential and critical message of the spiritual life is to share with and be supported by God and God's people. Pain without others becomes hell.

Suffering calls for compassion—to help others bear their pain. Our common ground of pain draws us together to accept, ease, and transcend our pain. When we are with people who care, our burdens are lighter and we become closer. Without spirituality, pain is something simply to treat or ameliorate.

Pain is also a magnet that draws us closer together. Pain strips us of our pretense and humbles us so that we can kneel down and look up for help. Our pain reminds us of our need for one another and for a caring reality that goes beyond suffering. Pain moves us to care and be cared for, to love and be loved by God, ourselves, and others. In this way, pain is a saving grace.

Elderly men and women, however, can become irritable and angry. For example, if they have repressed their anger, their dam of anger may burst and cause destruction. If they are accustomed to controlling situations, they may be frustrated and angry with their lack of control, or persist in trying to control. Some elderly are envious and jealous, and others are dependent and manipulative. Aging in itself is no cure for character defects. The redemptive processes of suffering love and compassion are severely tested by miserable old people who seem to try to make everyone else miserable. Our ministry is to rekindle their hidden spirits and affirm our being together in the Spirit.

A paradoxical phenomenon often occurs in the elder years: though our bodies look old, are old, and in many ways feel old, we can feel much younger and even "childlike." Instead of a childish regression to an earlier stage of development, we foster the open simplicity of an innocent child and the depth of a sage. Like the child, we live with a sense of surprise and exploration. Like the sage, we see with eyes of eternity.

Since many healthy elderly people manifest a childlikeness, an open simplicity, and a purity of the heart, they often play with children, and children often respond to them more openly than to other adults. Another reason may be that elderly people are less likely to be phony or engage in interpersonal games, but are more likely to present a light and warm spirit that manifests festive love. They appreciate the humor of existence and laugh with life.

An exciting feature of old age is that there is more time to play. The Spirit of play beckons us in our elder years. If our past has been an escape from play, the Spirit of play frightens us. Since we tend to choose activities that are most consistent with our past values and patterns, the ways that we prepare for play are important. If we have played consistently and authentically throughout life, play is a welcome activity that culminates in a light celebration of life. Without a playful spirit, we are usually sad and empty. Dancing with the Spirit of play, however, makes us gentle and happy.

Ageism, however, can make it difficult to celebrate the elder years. "We" perpetuate ageism by assuring that "they"—the elderly—are powerless, weak, dependent, and perhaps worthless. Medically, economically, and functionally, many may approximate this syndrome. But in other ways, and especially spiritually, they can be powerful, strong, autonomous, and full of worth. In fact, a paradoxical and uneasy saving grace is that happy elderly people intimidate "us"—those who are not elderly. Their being so close to death threatens us and, reacting in defense, we control and oppress them. Consequently, rather than learning from them, we teach them. Rather than listening, we talk about them and at them. Rather than caring for them, we treat them.

They intimidate us by exposing our unauthentic lives; they summon us to question our values. Because they intimidate us, we try to put them into categories—to make them all the same—"typical" of old age. Actually, empirical studies demonstrate that the elderly are the most diverse of all age groups. Even though we may not put many of them in geriatric facilities, we do minimize their value. Maybe these so-called old, weak, and powerless people can teach us something. Particularly those who are happy in being and who promote different values can indict our obsession with work, power, and success.

Consider, for example, how elderly people intimidate us by questioning our "quasi-living." Too often, we assume that we can live without death. We delude ourselves into thinking that death will someday happen, rather than realizing that death is always happening to us and not only to them. Since we are in fact beings-toward-death, we share their coming to death. Being close to death, elderly people proclaim the meaning of life. Rather than being intimidated, we can listen to them and let them help us.

The elderly can help us by refusing to play the game of being old, that is, dependent, silent, and worthless. They can proclaim themselves rather than silencing their truth. They can encounter us and even confront our normal madness. Rather than hiding from us, they can let themselves be seen and heard.

Elderly persons can also accept us and be compassionate. These warriors, who know what it means to battle life, can help us bear the burden of living a good life. And they can inspire us to seek what is best, rather than settling for anything less. They can also expect us to show them justice and respect. They can be friends who help us to grow old and face death. They can advise us on what to anticipate, how to cope, and how to transcend as well as advise us on economic, social, and interpersonal and personal matters. Most of all, they can be our mentors in spirituality.

We can also help them. Rather than denying death, we can face death in ourselves and, therefore, in them. We can come to the turning point when we no longer are intimidated but can listen to them. Becoming more aware of our living and dying, we can journey with them on their last trip. Both of us can come to accept and affirm that death is the final step in growth. We can thank each other, offer and ask for forgiveness, extend help, embrace in love, and finally bid fond farewell until we meet again.

But are we really open to the elderly, or do we subtly hide from them? For example, at a social gathering do we talk to the elderly for a few minutes, pat them on the head, excuse ourselves, and then return only when they need something? Instead of treating them as responsibilities, can we appreciate their superiority? Can we show genuine hospitality wherein we give them the space and time to be themselves? Are we there for them?

Can we become reconciled with the elderly, especially with those who have hurt us? Can we forgive—a giving that is always there with no strings attached? Do we share happiness with them rather than giving them projects to keep them happy? Do we motivate and challenge rather than reinforce their dependency? Do we invite them to be interdependent? Do we ask for their help?

Do we show delight with the elderly? Rather than being irritated with them, do we see them as being like us and show genuine care and concern? How often do we have genuine fun with them, celebrate with them, and truly enjoy them? Is being with the elderly a routine, a duty, a way of being nice, or of relieving our guilt? Do we condescend in our care? Can we truly listen to them? Do we get a "kick" out of them? Do we realize that the elderly are inexhaustible sources of faith, love, and hope?

So what if some do tell the same story several times; they never tell it in the same way. The information is not the primary factor, but rather the sharing and being with them. Though communication is helpful, communion is infinitely more important. Can we truly take in, support, and affirm the gift of their being? Rather than being resentful, can we be thankful that they are alive?

Can we show patience—a suffering and waiting in love? Can we move at their pace? Can we listen to their rhythm rather than forcing them to step to ours? Can we listen to their music and dance to their tune?

Do we understand elderly people? Can we enter into their world and appreciate their lives, or do we analyze and manipulate them? Do we see them as a problem to handle rather than a mystery to enjoy? Do we take the elderly for granted rather than having a deep sense of gratitude?

A paramount point is to face and heal the "we-them" dichotomy. Rather than being against each other, we can come together. We can affirm our common ground and become members of the same humankind. Can we see that we are different threads, new and old, of the same enduring tapestry? Can we let our spirits proclaim our common Spirit? Can we sing the songs and dance to the music of our Spirit? We can.

We need not propose a theory to justify being together, but rather we have to admit that our essential reality is being together. It is an old reality that must be rediscovered, rekindled, and lived. Whether or not we admit it, we have always shared in the same uncreated life force and depended on its power of Love. We can affirm that we are bound together by the Spirit of Life. We can rejoice in standing on the same ground. We can grow older together in God's Love.

Bibliography

Beattie, Melody. *Beyond Codependency.* San Francisco: A Harper/Hazelden Book, 1989.

Belsky, Janet. *The Adult Experience.* St. Paul, MN: West Publishing Co., 1997.

Butler, Robert. *Why Survive? Being Old in America.* New York: Harper and Row, 1975.

Chopra, Deepak. *The Spiritual Laws of Spiritual Success.* San Rafael, CA: New World Library, 1994.

Collins, Vincent C. *Acceptance.* St. Meinard, IN: Abbey Press, 1979.

Coward, Harold. (Ed.) *Life After Death in World Religions.* New York: The Crossroad Publishing Co., 1996.

Cummings, Charles. *Eco-Spirituality Toward a Reverent Life.* New York: Paulist Press, 1991.

Cummings, Charles. *Spirituality and the Desert Experience.* Denville, NJ: Dimension Books, 1978.

Dangott, Lillian R. and Richard A. Kalish. *A Time to Enjoy: The Pleasure of Aging.* Englewood Cliffs, NJ: Prentice-Hall, Inc., 1979.

Danielou, Jean. (Ed.) *From Glory to Glory: Texts from Gregory of Nyssa's Mystical Writings.* St. Vladimirs, 1979.

Davies, Oliver. *God Within: The Mystical Tradition of Northern Europe.* New York: Paulist Press, 1988.

DeMello, Anthony. *Awareness.* New York: Doubleday and Co., 1990.

Demm, Demetrius. *Flowers in the Desert.* New York: Paulist Press, 1987.

Doerff, Frances. *The Art of Passing Over.* New York: Paulist Press, 1988.

Downey, Michael. *Understanding Christian Spirituality.* New York: Paulist Press, 1997.

Erikson, Erik H. *Identity: Youth and Crisis.* New York: W.W. Norton and Co., 1968.

Evely, Louis. *Suffering.* New York: Herder and Herder, 1967.

Ferguson, Kitty. *The Fire in the Equations: Science, Religion, and the Search for God.* Grand Rapids, MI: William B. Eerdmans Publishing Co., 1994.

Fowler, John and Sam Keen. *Life Maps.* Waco, TX: Word Books, 1978.

Gilligan, Carol. *In a Different Voice.* Cambridge, MA: Harvard University Press, 1982.

Gould, Roger. *Transformations.* New York: Simon and Schuster, 1979.

Greeley, Andrew M. *When Life Hurts: Healing Themes from the Gospels.* Chicago: The Thomas Moore Press, 1988.

Hageman, Louise. *In the Midst of Winter.* Denville, NJ: Dimension Books, 1975.

Hall, Elizabeth. *Developmental Psychology Today,* Third Edition. New York: CRM/Random House, 1979.

Hamma, Robert M. *Along Your Desert Journey.* New York: Paulist Press, 1996.
Hammarskjold, Dag. *Markings*. Translated by Leif Sjoberg and W. H. Auden. New York: Alfred A. Knopf, Inc., 1964.
Heidegger, Martin. *Being and Time*. Translated by John Macquarrie and Edward Robinson. New York: Harper and Row, 1962.
Hendricks, Jon and C. Davis Hendricks. *Aging in Mass Society: Myths and Realities.* Cambridge, MA: Winthrop Publishers, Inc., 1977.
Hesse, Herman. *Siddhartha*. Translated by Hilda Rosner. New York: New Directions, 1951.
Hillman, James. *Blue Fire*. New York: Harper Perennial, 1989.
Hillman, James. *The Soul's Code*. New York: Random House, 1996.
Hulicka, Irene M. (Ed.) *Empirical Studies in the Psychology and Sociology of Aging.* New York: Thomas Y. Crowell Co., 1977.
Hurnard, Hannah. *Hinds' Feet on High Places.* Wheaton, IL: Living Books, 1987.
Huyck, Margaret Hellie. *Growing Older.* Englewood Cliffs, NJ: Prentice-Hall, Inc., 1974.
John Paul II. *Crossing the Threshold of Hope*. New York: Alfred A. Knopf, 1994.
Johnston, William. (Ed.) *The Cloud of Unknowing and the Book of Privy Counseling.* New York: Doubleday and Co., 1975.
Jones, Christopher. *Scott: A Meditation on Suffering and Helplessness.* Springfield, IL: Templegate Publishers, 1978.
Jung, Carl E. *Modern Man in Search of a Soul.* New York: Harcourt, Brace and Jovanovich, 1973.
Kalish, Richard A. *Late Adulthood, Perspective in Human Development.* Belmont, CA: Wadsworth Publishing Co., 1978.
Kavanaugh, Kiernan and Otilio Rodrigues. (Trans.) *The Collected Works of St. John of the Cross.* Washington, DC: ICS Publications, 1973.
Kavanaugh, Kiernan and Otilio Rodrigues. (Trans.) *Teresa of Avila: The Interior Castle.* New York: Paulist Press, 1979.
Kennedy, Carroll E. *Human Development: The Adult Years and Aging.* New York: Macmillan Publishing Co., Inc., 1978.
Kimmel, Douglas C. *Adulthood and Aging*. New York: John Wiley and Sons, Inc., 1974.
Kohlberg, Lawrence. "Stage and Sequence: The Cognitive-Developmental Approach of Socialization." In *Handbook of Socialization Theory,* D. A. Gostin (Ed.). Chicago: Rand McNally, 1969.
Kraft, William F. *Normal Modes of Madness*. New York: Alba House, 1978.
Kraft, William F. "Nothingness and Psychospiritual Growth," in *Review for Religious*, Vol. 37, No. 6, Nov., 1978.
Kraft, William F. *A Psychology of Nothingness*. Philadelphia: The Westminster Press, 1973.
Kraft, William F. *The Search for the Holy.* Philadelphia: The Westminster Press, 1971.
Kraft, William F. *Sexual Dimensions of the Celibate Life.* Kansas City, KS: Andrews and McMeel, 1979.

Kraft, William F. *Whole and Holy Sexuality.* St. Meinard, IN: Abbey Press, 1989.

Kreeft, Peter. *Making Sense Out of Suffering.* Ann Arbor, MI: Servant Books, 1986.

Kübler-Ross, Elisabeth. *Death: The Final Stage of Growth.* New York: Macmillan, 1975.

Kübler-Ross, Elisabeth. *On Death and Dying.* New York: The Macmillan Co., 1971.

Kung, Hans. (Ed.) *The Unknown God?* New York: Sheed and Ward, 1966.

Kurtz, Ernest. *The Spirituality of Imperfection: Storytelling and the Journey to Wholeness.* New York: Bantam Books, 1992.

Lawrence, Brother. *The Practice of the Presence of God.* Springdale, PA: Whitaker House, 1982.

Lerner, Harriet Goldham. *The Dance of Intimacy.* New York: Perennial Library, 1989.

Levinson, Daniel J. *The Seasons of a Man's Life.* New York: Alfred A. Knopf, 1978.

Lidz, Theodore. *The Person: His or Her Development Throughout the Cycle,* Revised Edition. New York: Basic Books, 1976.

Maloney, George. *God's Community of Love in the Indwelling Trinity.* Hyde Park, NY: New City Press, 1993.

Maloney, George. *On the Road to Perfection: Christian Humility in Modern Society.* Hyde Park, NY: New City Press, 1995.

Mason, James. (Ed.) *Healthy People 2000.* Boston: Jones and Bartlett Publishers, 1992.

May, Gerald G. *Addiction and Grace.* San Francisco: Harper and Row, 1989.

May, Rollo. *Love and Will.* New York: Dell Publishing Co., 1969.

Mayer, Nancy. *The Male Mid-Life Crisis: Fresh Start After 40.* New York: Doubleday and Co., 1978.

McNamara, William. *Mystical Passion: Spirituality for a Bored Society.* Mahwah, NJ: Paulist Press, 1970.

Merton, Thomas. *Contemplation in a World of Action.* New York: Doubleday and Co., 1979.

Merton, Thomas. *Seeds of Contemplation.* New York: Doubleday and Co., 1971.

Moore, Thomas. *Care of the Soul.* New York: HarperCollins, 1992.

Moore, Thomas. *Soul Mates.* New York: HarperCollins, 1994.

Nemeck, Frances Kelly and Marie Theresa Coombs. *O Blessed Night.* New York: Alba House, 1991.

Neugarton, Bernice L. (Ed.) *Middle Age and Aging.* Chicago: University of Chicago Press, 1968.

Niland, Sherwin. *The Way We Die: Reflections on Life's Final Chapter.* New York: A. Knopf, 1994.

Nouwen, Henri J. M. *The Inner Voice of Love: A Journey Through Anguish to Freedom.* New York: Doubleday and Co., 1996.

Nouwen, Henri J. M. *The Wounded Healer: Ministry in Contemporary Society.* New York: Doubleday and Co., 1972.

Novak, Michael. *The Experience of Nothingness.* New York: Harper and Row, 1970.

O'Collins, Gerald. *The Second Journey: Spiritual Awareness and the Mid-Life Crisis.* New York: Paulist Press, 1978.

O'Murphy, Diarmuid. *Quantum Theology: Spiritual Implications of the New Physics.* New York: Crossroad, 1997.

O'Shea, Donagh. *I Remember Your Name in the Night: Thinking About Death.* Mystic, CT: Twenty-Third Publications, 1997.

Paul, Margaret. *Inner Bonding.* San Francisco: Harper and Row, 1990.

Peck, Scott. *Further Along the Road Less Traveled: The Legendary Journey Toward Spiritual Growth.* New York: Simon and Schuster, 1993.

Peck, Scott. *The Road Less Traveled.* New York: Simon and Schuster, 1978.

Pollard, Miriam. *The Other Face of Love: Dialogues with the Prison Experience of Albert Speer.* New York: The Crossroad Publishing Co., 1996.

Rahner, Karl. *On the Theology of Death.* New York: Herder and Herder, 1961.

Royda, Crose. *Why Women Live Longer Than Men.* San Francisco: Jossey-Bass Publications, 1997.

Russell, Jeffrey Burton. *A History of Heaven.* Princeton, NJ: Princeton University Press, 1997.

Sardello, Robert. *Facing the World with Soul.* New York: Harper Perennial, 1994.

Seifert, Kevin, Robert J. Hoffnung, and Michelle Hoffnung. *Lifespan Development.* Boston: Houghton-Mifflin Co., 1997.

Sheehy, Gail. *New Passages: Mapping Your Life Across Time.* New York: Random House, 1995.

Sheehy, Gail. *Passages: Predictable Crises of Adult Life.* New York: Dutton and Co., Inc., 1974.

Sheehy, Gail. *Pathfinders.* New York: Boston Books, 1982.

Sheehy, Gail. *The Silent Passage.* New York: Pocket Books, 1991.

Simmons, Henry C. *In the Footsteps of the Mystics.* New York: Paulist Press, 1992.

Taylor, John V. *The Go-Between God.* Philadelphia: Fortress Press, 1973.

Tuoti, Frank X. *Why Not Be a Mystic?* New York: The Crossroad Publishing Co., 1995.

Tyrrell, Thomas. *Urgent Longings.* Mystic, CT: Twenty-Third Publications, 1994.

Underhill, Evelyn. *Mysticism: A Study in the Nature and Development of Man's Spiritual Consciousness.* New York: E.P. Dutton and Company, 1971.

Vaillant, George. *Adaptation to Life.* Boston: Little, Brown and Co., 1977.

Van Croonenberg, Bert. *Don't Be Discouraged.* Denville, NJ: Dimension Books, Inc., 1972.

Van Kaam, Adrian. *The Transcendent Self: The Formative Spirituality of Middle, Early and Later Years of Life.* Denville, NJ: Dimension Books, Inc., 1979.

Weil, Simone. *Waiting for God.* Translated by Emma Crawford, New York: Harper-Collins, 1973.

Whitehead, Evelyn E. and James D. Whitehead. *Christian Life Patterns: The Psychological Challenges and Religious Invitations of Adult Life.* New York: Doubleday and Co., 1979.

Willhite, Thomas D. *Living Synergistically.* San Rafael, CA: PSI World, 1975.

Wojtyla, Karol. *Sign of Contradiction.* New York: The Seabury Press, 1979.

Wuthnow, Robert. *Sharing and the Journey.* New York: The Free Press, 1994.

Young-Eisendrath, Polly. *The Gift of Suffering: Finding Insight, Compassion, and Renewal.* New York: Addison-Wesley Publishing Co., Inc., 1996.

Index